ACCLAIM FOR

THE GREEK YOGURT KITCHEN

"I love Greek yogurt, a t! These recipes are creative, flavorful, and ishes using a newer, healthier approach to cc

bestselling author of *The Pound a Day Diet*

"This cookbook celebra nd delicious addition to everyday dishes such n fingers, or in place of some of the fat in pa hole family will love these healthy and delici ne!"

Missy Chase Lapine, aky Chef cookbooks

"What a fabulous and Toby entices readers by showcasing every de , nutrients, and endless versatility. She help lescribes the creamy food's role in your hea yogurt–based icing on the cake? By includ er, and dessert (yes, frosting too!), Toby pro food in *every* meal of the day."

s *Quick Fix Meals* and author of *The Robin Takes 5 Cookbook for Busy Families*

"Toby highlights the expansive use of Greek yogurt in a wide array of wholesome, scrumptious recipes. She takes an in-depth look at the health benefits of this fantastic ingredient and provides tips and tricks for making Greek yogurt part of a healthy lifestyle. This cookbook is a wonderful addition to any healthy recipe collection!"

—Cheryl Forberg, RD, *New York Times* bestselling author, James Beard award–winning chef and nutritionist, and culinary consultant for NBC's *The Biggest Loser*

"Dairy up! Toby Amidor has created the perfect way to add more dairy to your life, while lightening up your meals and your waistline, too. She shows us how to use the delicious creaminess of Greek yogurt to add so much flavor, and oh, by the way, nutritional goodness, to your meals and snacks. Dairy has been shown to help you reach and maintain a healthy weight; it helps improve blood pressure and build muscle; and yogurt is especially good for healthy digestion. Toby gives us the most delicious cookbook for your whole family, and happens to sneak in good health along with great taste."

—Marla Heller, *New York Times* bestselling author of *The Dash Diet Weight Loss Solution*

"As a self-proclaimed Greek yogurt addict, this book is heaven. Toby has thought of everything you can possibly do with rich and creamy yogurt, and her creative, mouthwatering recipes will knock your socks off!"

—Joy Bauer, MS, RD, CDN, bestselling author and nutrition/health expert for NBC's *Today* show

THE GREEK YOGURT KITCHEN

MORE THAN 130 DELICIOUS, HEALTHY RECIPES FOR EVERY MEAL OF THE DAY

TOBY AMIDOR,
MS, RD, CDN

Grand Central Life & Style
Hachette Book Group
237 Park Avenue
New York, NY 10017

www.GrandCentralLifeandStyle.com

Printed in the United States of America

RRD-C

First Edition: May 2014
10 9 8 7 6 5 4 3 2 1

Grand Central Life & Style is an imprint of Grand Central Publishing.
The Grand Central Life & Style name and logo are trademarks of Hachette Book Group, Inc.

Library of Congress Cataloging-in-Publication Data has been applied for.

ISBN: 978-1-4555-5120-0 (pbk.)—ISBN: 978-1-4555-5119-4 (ebook)

To my children, Schoen, Ellena, and Micah.
Always remember that hard work, passion, and dedication
will enable you to achieve your dreams.
I love you.

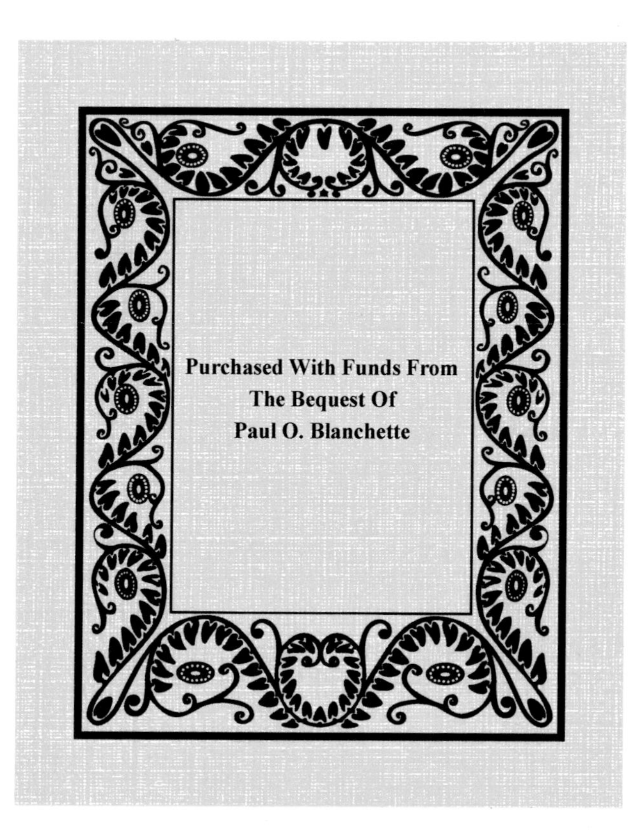

Acknowledgments

There are many people I want to thank for making this book possible. Thank you to my husband, Eilon, for being understanding and patient during my trials and tribulations when attempting to balance family and work. My dad, Henry Oksman, always taught me that you can achieve anything and everything with hard work, desire, and dedication. I thank you every day for this lifelong lesson. My mom, Zipporah Oksman, taught me the importance of cooking and thinking outside the box when developing recipes. It was an honor to graduate from New York University alongside you as we both earned our nutrition degrees. I thank you for these life lessons and experiences.

Thank you to Dalyn Miller and Holly Schmidt at Hollan Publishing, who truly brought this project to life. A huge thank-you to my editor, Amanda Englander at Grand Central Publishing, who made my experience writing this cookbook an easy and enjoyable one. It was an honor to work with you. I am overwhelmed and flattered by the dedication and hard work that each member of my team put into this cookbook. Thank you so much, Melissa O'Shea, MS, RD; Gail Watson-Brown, MS; Gena Seraita, RD, CDN; and Mary Opfer, MS, RD, CDN.

Thank you for your continued support and encouragement, my fellow nutrition friends: Dana Angelo White, MS, RD, ATC; Ellie Krieger, MS, RD; Stacey Jackson, MS, RD; Melissa Halas-Liang, MA, RD, CDE; and Rachel Begun, MS, RDN. Lastly, thank you to my wonderful and supportive family, who were my dedicated taste testers, bearing with me through my crazy schedule: my children, Schoen, Ellena, and Micah; my siblings, Benjamin,

Tahneer, Jacob, and Maurice Oksman; my sibling-in-laws, Dana Oksman and Jonathan Waldauer; and my grandparents, Hannah Schoenberger, Rachel Oksman, and Alexander Krayzman. And to my in-laws, Mira and Avi Amidor, who gave me support from Israel via Skype.

Contents

Introduction

May 16, 2002, was the most memorable day of my life. I walked into White Plains Hospital at 6:00 a.m., and by 2:25 p.m., I had given birth to my pride and joy, my first child, Schoen. Once he was off to the nursery, I settled into my post-delivery room in the maternity wing and realized that giving birth gives you a heck of an appetite. Luckily, shortly after this realization my mother walked in with a bag full of freshly purchased snacks. She sat down next to me and pulled out a small white container labeled "Greek yogurt with honey." May 16, 2002, was also the first day I tried Greek yogurt—and it was love at first bite.

After Schoen and I returned home from the hospital, I called my mother to find out where I could pick up that fantastic yogurt. I soon learned that only two stores near me sold it! Each week I would stock up on the little white containers with honey packed on the side. It quickly became my daily go-to snack. And since I was nursing, I was thrilled that my delicious new snack was full of protein and calcium. After one year, I stopped nursing Schoen, and as many new moms do, decided it was time to focus on losing those last ten pounds of baby weight. My daily dose of thick, creamy Greek yogurt had been the full-fat variety, and it didn't take a rocket scientist to figure out that I needed to cut down on calories in order to shed the weight. But as a trained clinical dietitian and a foodie, I wanted to do it in a healthy way with wholesome, delicious food. Luckily, low-fat Greek yogurt started popping up more frequently on store shelves, though they didn't always have the honey packed on the side. So I started experimenting with my own toppings like sliced strawberries, grapes, almonds, granola, and of course, honey.

Just a few years later, nonfat plain Greek yogurt overtook store shelves. Around the same time, I began realizing that most of the traditional low-calorie yogurts were filled with artificial sweeteners and a laundry list of ingredients—many of which I didn't recognize. The ingredient list for the Greek yogurt was much cleaner, with few ingredients, which is what I look for in food. Flavored Greek yogurt soon followed, and that inspired me to begin experimenting with smoothies. As I was making my breakfast smoothie one morning, I decided to swap my traditional yogurt for Greek—and boy, was I delighted with the results! Strawberry Greek yogurt combined with cranberry juice and frozen strawberries quickly became one of my favorites, and now has become the smoothie of choice for my three little ones.

It is no surprise that the popularity of this super-food has exploded since Schoen was born more than eleven years ago. Store shelves are lined with a wide variety of flavors, tubs in every size, and snack packs with much more than just honey on the side. The tangy, luscious taste of Greek yogurt has gone far beyond everyday snack food. It even appeared at the most recent Olympic Games, fueling athletes! Because I am now in the media, I receive many food samples, including Greek yogurt. I have tasted many of the newly created flavors, blends, and tubes, and have taste-tested them with my own kids. My eight-year-old daughter, Ellena, is now a big fan of nonfat vanilla Greek yogurt and tops it with cereal and strawberries—talk about being a proud dietitian mom!

As I was writing this book, Ellena was always peering over my shoulder, asking what I was cooking next. She was my avid taste tester throughout the entire process. I really wanted this book to showcase the versatility of the delicious food that has become a staple ingredient in my own kitchen. Through my continued curiosity and experimentation, I have found that Greek yogurt is the perfect replacement for higher-fat ingredients like cream cheese, mayonnaise, oil, butter, sour cream, buttermilk, and heavy cream. I use it for everything from smoothies, parfaits, dips, dressings, and marinades to mashed potatoes, muffins, cakes, breads, and cookies. I have even learned to incorporate Greek yogurt into my favorite comfort foods, like pancakes, egg salad, pizza, and brownies, as well as more classic dishes like penne bolognese and clafoutis, where Greek yogurt can add flavor and texture. And as a dietitian, I love the fact that it's a nutrition powerhouse contributing twice the amount of protein per ounce than traditional yogurt. Plus, it is a good source of calcium, which helps strengthen the bones and teeth of my growing children.

So why did I create *more than 130 recipes*? It's 133 to be exact! The number 13 has brought me much luck in the past and hopefully will bring me luck in the future, too. Each of the 133 recipes was carefully selected to show the versatility of Greek yogurt and to help highlight simple ways it can be incorporated into what are already your favorite dishes. We all lead hectic lives and are always pressed for time; these recipes are easy to follow and use many wholesome ingredients like fruits, vegetables, whole grains, nuts, seeds, low-fat and nonfat dairy, and lean proteins. Sodium and cholesterol are also kept in check and there are no artificial sweeteners in sight.

Each recipe contains exact measurements for a serving size. I always find this information useful not only to help keep an eye on calories but also to allow me to purchase items only in the quantities needed—a well-written shopping list with specific quantities can actually lower your grocery bill. I find this trick especially helpful when purchasing pricier items such as meat, fish, poultry, and cheese. A nutrition breakdown is also available for each recipe, listing calories, total fat, saturated fat, protein, total carbohydrates, sugars, fiber, cholesterol, and sodium to help you always make the best decisions for your individual needs.

I hope you take the concepts in this cookbook far beyond the 133 recipes provided and make your own kitchen a Greek yogurt kitchen. I truly believe that every bite of the food we choose to eat should be savored and enjoyed.

Happy, healthy cooking!

CHAPTER 1

Greek Yogurt: A Superstar Food

THE RISE TO FAME

Greek yogurt has found a place in the hearts of Americans, and it is no surprise. This beloved food is considered to be one of the fastest-growing on the market. In 2009, Greek yogurt represented 3% of the U.S. yogurt market. By 2011, it was up to 16%, and just one year later had skyrocketed to 28%![1] According to a report released by Packaged Facts titled *The Yogurt Market and Yogurt Innovation: Greek Yogurt and Beyond*, retail dollar sales of Greek yogurt in the U.S. market increased more than 50% in 2012 to reach $1.6 billion.[2]

Today grocery store shelves are lined with different brands and varieties of Greek yogurt. While this market is growing rapidly, usually two or three of the most popular brands overwhelm store shelves with their many varieties. Several lesser-known brands of Greek yogurt will usually be sprinkled on store shelves, too. And it's not only the dairy aisle that's expanding! You can now find many products made with Greek yogurt, such as smoothies, frozen yogurt, butter, cream cheese, hummus, guacamole, salad dressings, dips and spreads, and granola bars. With its thick, creamy texture, versatility in the kitchen, and ample protein (double the protein of traditional yogurt), it has gained super-food status. But exactly how did it become one of the fastest-growing food categories of all time?

Greek yogurt—also known as strained yogurt—is made using the centuries-old technique of straining out the watery liquid (or whey) in yogurt, resulting in a thicker, richer, and tangier product. Traditionally the straining is all it takes—no gums, thickeners, or milk fats are added to thicken the yogurt. Although you may think it originated in Greece, it didn't! First, let's take a look at how traditional yogurt came about. The word "yogurt" comes from the Turkish word meaning to "thicken" or "curdle." Many history books attribute the discovery of yogurt to an accident around 6000 BCE, when the Neolithic peoples of Central Asia began the practice of milking their domesticated animals. The milk was likely stored and carried in bags made from the animals' stomachs, which contained natural enzymes. The enzymes curdled the milk, thereby creating yogurt, which lasted longer and had a delicious tangy flavor. In the 1700s, Turkish immigrants brought yogurt to North America, but it really didn't catch on until the 1940s, when it began to be mass-produced in a factory in the Bronx, New York.

But the Turks weren't the only ones eating yogurt. For thousands of years yogurt has been a popular food in the Middle East, and it has become a staple in the Eastern European diet. Africa, India, and the Arab countries have traditional cultured-milk dishes, several of which are created by straining yogurt. *Labneh*, popular in Arab countries, is a strained yogurt commonly used in sandwiches. *Mishti dahi* is an East Indian dessert created by boiling strained yogurt in large containers so that the liquid content is reduced to a thick, custard-like yogurt. *Tzatziki* is a dip or sauce made with strained yogurt, cucumbers, garlic, olive oil, and salt, served in Greek cuisine.

Although we do know that strained yogurt is part of numerous food cultures around the world, the exact origin is unclear. The confusion really stems from the term "Greek," which actually describes how the yogurt was processed—by straining—as opposed to the country of origin.

But whatever the origin may be, the mounting popularity of Greek yogurt in the United States is undeniable. And as the saying goes, "Timing is everything." The introduction of Greek yogurt into the United States coincided with the rise in popularity of farmers markets as well as the slow and local food movements. People today are craving purer, simpler, and more natural foods. Greek yogurt has come to the rescue. Its boom has also come at a time when gluten-free and low-carb foods are all the rage—both categories it fits into. You can now find Greek yogurt—plain, flavored, and packaged in a variety of ways—in markets throughout the United States. It is shelved in the refrigerated dairy aisle, usually right next to the traditional yogurt we've seen for years. So what makes Greek yogurt the better choice?

GREEK VS. TRADITIONAL YOGURT

As discussed, Greek yogurt is less watery than traditional yogurt because it is strained to remove the whey. The removal of whey also results in less sugar, fewer carbohydrates, more protein, and less lactose. It leads to a thicker, creamier consistency and a rich flavor. It also helps boost the nutrition status. Let's take a look at the numbers.[3]

	Greek yogurt, nonfat plain (6-ounce single-serving container)	*Traditional yogurt, nonfat plain (6-ounce single-serving container)*
Calories	87	95
Total Fat (grams)	0.5	0.3
Cholesterol (milligrams)	7	2
Sodium (milligrams)	53	77
Sugar (grams)	4.8	8
Protein (grams)	15	6
Calcium (percent daily recommended amount)	16	33

*Note: Nutrition facts vary from brand to brand, so be sure to read the label.

As you can see, Greek yogurt has 38% less sodium, 40% less sugar, and more than twice the amount of protein than traditional yogurt. In 2010, the United States Department of Agriculture's Dietary Guidelines for Americans recommended a maximum of 2,300 milligrams of sodium per day. For folks more than 50 years of age or anyone who has diabetes, high blood pressure, or chronic kidney disease, the recommended limit was set at 1,500 milligrams.[4] With 38% less sodium, Greek yogurt is a better option to help keep your daily sodium intake in check.

When it comes to sugar, Greek yogurt is the hands-down winner. Fruit-flavored Greek yogurt typically has around 2 to 3 teaspoons more sugar per serving than plain. Traditional fruit-flavored yogurt has around 5 teaspoons more, but that can vary depending on the brand. Much of that extra sugar, in both types of yogurt, comes from processed sugars like fructose and evaporated cane sugar. Many traditional yogurt brands use artificial sweeteners instead to cut calories, but I recommend avoiding those as much as possible. I don't like to put anything artificial in my body on a regular basis, and would never feed artificially sweetened foods to my kids. If you're looking for a natural sweetener, opt for honey-flavored Greek yogurt instead. Just be aware that a few honey-flavored varieties tend to have more sugar per serving than fruit-sweetened varieties. I do recommend choosing yogurt with natural sweeteners like honey, as honey contains small amounts of vitamins and minerals like iron, riboflavin, niacin, potassium, and zinc. Just be sure to compare labels in order to select the honey-flavored Greek yogurt with the least amount of added sugar. All of that said, though, the plain traditional varieties contain no added sugar, just like plain Greek yogurt.

Thanks to the straining process, a good amount of lactose is removed from Greek yogurt, making it a lactose intolerant–friendly food. Less lactose does also mean less calcium, but Greek yogurt still provides an ideal quantity to help you meet the recommended daily amount.

To put it simply, although both traditional and Greek yogurt can be part of a healthful diet, Greek yogurt contains less junk. Many brands of traditional yogurt include thickeners, stabilizers, artificial coloring, and processed sweeteners. There is one caveat, though: While the majority of Greek yogurt brands use the traditional straining process to create their luscious taste, a handful do use added gums, thickeners, and milk fats to create the thick and creamy texture Greek yogurt is famous for. The method by which a brand creates that rich Greek yogurt texture has been a source of controversy. Several well-known Greek yogurt brands take pride in creating their yogurt using traditional straining. This lengthy process requires specialized equipment and therefore the yogurt costs more to produce, which means it will cost you more at the store. Other companies cut corners and use inexpensive additives in order to achieve that thick and creamy consistency, and these brands are able to sell Greek yogurt at a lower price. Always be sure to check the nutrition facts and ingredient list before purchasing. Ingredients like xanthan gum, locust bean gum, and cornstarch are usually red flags indicating that thickeners have been added to create a thick and creamy texture.

THE HEALTH BENEFITS

Healthy, popular, and delicious are not the only attributes of this super-food. Greek yogurt has been touted for its many health benefits in digestive health, heart health, weight control, bone health, diabetes, and lactose intolerance.

Probiotics and Digestive Health

In addition to boasting the better nutritional profile, Greek yogurt also provides many health benefits that you won't find in traditional yogurt. One of the most touted of these is Greek yogurt's probiotics, that is, healthy bacteria, which help promote a healthy gut. Your digestive tract is constantly flooded with bacteria—some of it good, helping to break down food, and some of it harmful, causing illness. The digestive tract can handle only a certain number of bacteria at one time. Eating Greek yogurt with probiotics helps increase the good bacteria in your gut—and the more good bacteria you take in, the less room there is for the bad. These friendly bacteria can help keep you regular and fight bad bacteria that may cause diarrhea. Probiotics can also be beneficial for those who suffer from irritable bowel syndrome and several other intestinal diseases, such as Crohn's disease and ulcerative colitis. Researchers believe that some digestive disorders occur when the balance of the good bacteria in the gut is disturbed, or when the lining of the intestines becomes damaged; probiotics help keep the friendly bacteria in check and protect the integrity of the gut. These good bacteria can also help *treat* such intestinal disorders, as well as alleviate travelers' diarrhea, the diarrhea you may get from taking antibiotics, and some of the symptoms associated with allergic reactions. Probiotics have been shown to help enhance the immune system by increasing the number of T cells, which defend your body from invaders and decrease the occurrence of yeast infections. Studies have also found that T cells can help prevent certain types of cancer, especially colon cancer.[5]

With so many benefits, probiotics should be a regular part of a healthy eating plan. So how do you find them? Probiotics appear under the ingredient list on the nutrition facts panel. The ones most commonly used in Greek yogurt are lactobacillus, streptococcus, and bifidobacterium. They are abbreviated as "L," "S," and "B" followed by the species name. You can look for *S. thermophilus*, *L. bulgaricus*, *L. acidophilus*, and *L. casei*. Or, if that gave you a headache, another way to determine whether there are probiotics in your Greek yogurt is to look for the words "live and active cultures" at the end of the ingredient list, or to look for the "live and active cultures" seal on the packaging. The approval seal was developed by the National Yogurt Association to help identify yogurt products containing significant amounts of live and active cultures, and can be used on any yogurt that contained at least 100 million cultures per gram at the time it was manufactured. The seal is voluntary, though, so some yogurts may contain live cultures but not say so. (You can also find probiotics in cheese, miso, kefir, sauerkraut, and kimchi.)

High Blood Pressure and Heart Health

About 1 in 3 U.S. adults has high blood pressure,[6] which can lead to damage of the arteries, heart, brain, and lungs. One of the main recommendations to help control blood pressure is diet: The National Heart, Lung, and Blood Pressure Institute (NHLBI) recommends following the DASH (Dietary Approaches to Stop Hypertension) diet. This plan is low in fat, and includes 8 to 10 servings of fruits and vegetables and 2 to 3 servings of low-fat or nonfat dairy products each day. Dairy is an important source of calcium, potassium, and magnesium and studies have found that these three minerals may help to lower high blood pressure.[7] But instead of popping supplements, I recommend eating real foods high in these minerals—like Greek yogurt.

Many studies have also confirmed the link between eating low- and nonfat dairy products and a lower risk of heart attacks and stroke: A 2011 study published in the American *Journal of Clinical Nutrition* looked at more than 1,000 older women to see the effect milk, yogurt, and cheese had on plaque buildup in the arteries. The women who ate yogurt regularly were found to have the least plaque buildup, meaning they had a lower risk for heart attack and stroke.[8] A 2006 study published in *Hypertension* followed close to 5,000 people in the National Heart, Lung, and Blood Institute Family Heart Study. They found that folks who ate more low-fat dairy foods had lower blood pressure, putting them at lower risk for heart attacks and stroke.[9] A 2005 study published in the *American Journal of Clinical Nutrition* found a 50% reduction in the risk of developing high blood pressure in folks who ate 2 to 3 servings of low-fat dairy every day.[10] Although this study focused mainly on milk, researchers on the study believe low-fat yogurt would most likely provide the same benefits. So the heart-healthy benefits are clear!

Weight

What else can Greek yogurt do? Many people are looking to lose weight and seek a magic food that will help them do so. Although there is no one food that will melt the fat away—sorry!—many studies have linked eating dairy products with weight loss. A 2010 study published in the *American Journal of Clinical Nutrition* compared 300 men and women who followed either a low-fat, Mediterranean, or low-carb diet over a 2-year period. Regardless of the type of diet being followed, folks who ate the most dairy (equivalent to about 2 glasses of milk per day) lost approximately 12 pounds more than folks who ate a low amount of dairy (equivalent to ½ cup of milk per day).[11]

So why *is* Greek yogurt better for weight loss than other dairy products? Because it's so much higher in protein. Since protein takes longer for the body to digest, it helps keep you feeling fuller longer. Feeling full and satisfied is especially important if you're trying to lose weight, since it can help minimize those extra snack cravings. There is indeed evidence that yogurt specifically aids in weight loss. A 2006 study published in the *International Journal of Obesity* found that obese people who ate yogurt daily over the course of 3 months lost more body fat while maintaining lean tissue than those who did not eat yogurt every day. Those eating yogurt also lost more inches around their waist.[12]

Including dairy foods in your diet can also help *prevent* weight gain. A 2006 study published in *Obesity* found that young, normal-weight women who ate 1,300 to 1,400 milligrams of calcium per day from dairy foods over 18 months gained less body fat compared with women who did not. Researchers concluded that adding more calcium from dairy foods may help prevent weight gain in young, healthy women.[13]

While you don't want to overdose on Greek yogurt by eating endless amounts, I recommended including 1 or 2 single-serving containers of nonfat plain Greek yogurt each day when you're trying to lose weight or to maintain a healthy weight.

Bone Health

As we age, our bones naturally become thinner—and as our bones become thinner, they lose calcium and other minerals faster, becoming less dense and more porous, making them more vulnerable to breaks. Over time, low bone density can lead to osteoporosis. According to the National Osteoporosis Foundation, about 9 million Americans have this disease and about 48 million have low bone density. To put these numbers into perspective: That means that 6 out of every 10 adults 50 years and older are at risk of breaking a bone, especially in the hip, spine, and wrist. That's a pretty scary statistic.

So how does Greek yogurt help? It provides important nutrients—including calcium, magnesium, phosphorus, potassium, and protein—that work together to protect your bones. A study conducted at Washington University School of Medicine found that taking in calcium from dairy foods rather than from calcium supplements had a more positive impact on bone mineral density in postmenopausal women.[14] Because dairy foods influence bone health and even prevent osteoporosis later in life, it is important to eat the daily recommended 3 servings of low-fat or nonfat dairy products each day as part of a healthy diet.

But it's not just older folks who should be paying attention to their bones. Young children must also meet their dairy recommendations every day. The National Institute of Child Health and Human Development recommends that children and teenagers take in an equivalent of 4 cups of milk each day from low-fat and nonfat milk and dairy products in order to help build strong bones and reduce the risk of osteoporosis later in life.[15] The report stresses the importance of adults modeling such behavior in order to help young kids build good habits starting at an early age. With the higher protein content that kids need to grow and develop, Greek yogurt is an ideal dairy food to add to a child's diet.

Diabetes

There's also evidence that taking in low-fat and nonfat dairy foods, including Greek yogurt, can help decrease the risk of type 2 diabetes. During the U.S. Women's Health Study, researchers examined the eating habits of more than 37,000 women over a 10-year period. The results showed that women who ate the most dairy (close to 3 servings each day) had a 21% lower risk for type 2 diabetes compared to those who ate less than about ¾ serving of dairy each day. For every extra serving of dairy food eaten, there was a 4% lower risk of type 2 diabetes.[16] Other studies have found similar results in men, with each extra serving of dairy food reducing the risk of diabetes by 9%.[17] With its high protein content, Greek yogurt is a better choice for diabetics. It helps slow down the absorption of sugar into the blood—and having better blood sugar control is crucial for managing the disease.

Lactose Intolerance

Lactose intolerance is a sensitivity to the milk sugar called *lactose*. Its exact prevalence is unknown since many folks self-diagnose or decide they should be on a lactose-free diet. Symptoms of lactose intolerance include bloating, gas, abdominal discomfort, and diarrhea after drinking milk or ingesting milk products that contain lactose. These symptoms come about when a person has a hard time digesting the natural sugar (lactose) found in milk. A milk *allergy* occurs when the body's immune system rejects the protein found in milk. Being lactose intolerant is *not* the same as having a milk allergy. Symptoms of a milk allergy may include hives, vomiting, wheezing, diarrhea, abdominal cramps, itchy nose, and watery eyes. An allergic reaction is triggered by the immune system, whereas the symptoms of lactose intolerance are triggered by the digestive system.

But here's the thing most people don't realize: Being lactose intolerant does not mean you should be avoiding milk and dairy foods completely. Only when a person is *allergic* to dairy do they need to avoid all dairy products completely. Studies have shown that those with lactose intolerance can tolerate up to 12 grams of lactose at one time—the amount of lactose found in 1 cup of milk. The amount of lactose tolerated isn't affected by the fat content, so the 1 cup can be whole milk, nonfat, 1%—whatever you like. Many folks either misdiagnose themselves with a milk allergy or unnecessarily avoid all dairy products because of their lactose intolerance. But by avoiding milk and dairy products, they are missing out on the nutritional, health, and cooking advantages. A physician can help determine if you do have lactose intolerance by conducting a test, such as a lactose tolerance test or a hydrogen breath test.

If you are indeed lactose intolerant, it is still important to meet the recommended 3 servings of dairy each day. The amount of lactose each person can tolerate is different, so turning to dairy foods with less lactose is a good first step. Greek yogurt contains a lower amount of lactose because the straining process removes much of it. While traditional yogurt contains 13 grams of lactose per cup, Greek yogurt contains only 4 grams, making it a perfect dairy food for lactose intolerants! The table below shows the amount of lactose in common dairy foods.

AMOUNT OF LACTOSE IN COMMON DAIRY FOODS	
Food	*Lactose (grams)*
Whole, 2%, 1%, skim milk (1 cup)	12
Yogurt, traditional, low-fat, plain (6 ounces)	13
Yogurt, Greek, nonfat, plain (6 ounces)	**4**
Ice cream, vanilla, light, no sugar added (½ cup)	4
Cottage cheese, low-fat, 2% milk fat (½ cup)	3
American cheese, pasteurized, processed (1 ounce)	1
Cheddar cheese, sharp (1 ounce)	<0.1
Swiss cheese (1 ounce)	<0.1
Mozzarella cheese (1 ounce)	<0.1
Lactose-free low-fat milk	0

*Note: These averages are supplied by the USDA. Lactose content varies by product and the lactose content of a specific product would need to be verified by a vendor. Unless otherwise indicated, data sourced from: USDA / ARS, Nutrient Data Laboratory, Standard Reference. Found: August 2013. Lactose content based on sugar content when lactose alone was not available.

Alternative milks like soy, almond, rice, and hemp are all lactose-free since they are not made from cow's milk; however, these milks don't contain as many nutrients as cow's milk or products made from cow's milk. There are also a wide variety of lactose-free products available including milk, cottage cheese, and ice cream. These are made from cow's milk, but the lactose is broken down so the person eating them doesn't experience any uncomfortable symptoms after consuming them. Lactose-free dairy products can be used anywhere you find milk, including in cooking and baking, and have the same nutrient profile as their lactose-filled counterparts. Butter, with virtually no lactose, is another fine choice for those with lactose intolerance (in moderation of course). Cheese is also low in lactose. The issue there is that those extremely delicious cheeses tend to be high in fat, cholesterol, and sodium. In order to use cheese healthfully, you can incorporate a small amount of very flavorful varieties. That way, the recipe remains lactose-friendly and tasty.

Another strategy for easing digestion of dairy foods is to eat lactose-containing food together with other foods. For example, top a bowl of lentil soup with a dollop of nonfat Greek yogurt, or add 2 tablespoons of low-fat plain Greek yogurt to a meat sauce. The combination of any food with dairy helps slow digestion, giving the body more time to digest lactose. Just don't think that being lactose intolerant means you have to miss out on all the deliciousness of milk, yogurt, and cheese. By slowly adding lower-lactose foods like Greek yogurt into your diet, you can build up the body's ability to handle lactose. So the next time you go food shopping, add Greek yogurt to your cart!

Snacking for Health

Many folks don't understand how important snacking really is. Though snacks have gained a bad reputation for leading to weight gain and unhealthy eating habits, a healthy eating plan includes one to two snacks each day. It is not the act of snacking, but rather poor snacking habits and unhealthy snack choices that can lead to such issues. Munching on a bag of chips or cookies in front of the television in the evening is a poor snacking habit: Neither provides any nutritional goodness and the portions are well beyond the smart calorie range. To be effective, a snack should range between 125 and 250 calories and consist of several good-for-you nutrients like fiber, protein, vitamins, and minerals. This is why it is important to be conscious of what you snack on, when you snack, and where you snack. Many folks often underestimate the number of calories in their snacks, especially when choosing so-called healthy foods. One study found that when cookies were labeled "organic," people thought they were munching on 40% fewer calories than the same cookies without that label.[18] Clearly, it's critical to read the nutrition facts carefully and pay attention to serving sizes!

Don't be surprised that snacks are an important part of a healthy eating plan. You can think of them as mini meals that provide nourishment and help prevent hunger and stray grazing between meals. Every time we eat, our blood sugar goes up. Then, as we continue our day—walking, running, talking, and doing our everyday activities—our blood sugar drops back down. If blood sugar goes too low, it can result in a late-afternoon energy slump—or even worse, a bad craving for sugary foods. Eating a balanced snack helps maintain that blood sugar level between meals. If you find yourself going 5 or more hours between meals, add a snack during that time frame. It also helps you take in all the nutrients needed to maintain a healthy body. The foods we choose at every meal *should* provide us with everything we need, but that doesn't always happen. If some of these important nutrients can be eaten during snack time, there is less pressure to get them in during meals. And if some important nutrients are lacking in your diet (like fiber, iron, folate, calcium, or vitamin C), snacks are the perfect opportunity to get them in. Other benefits of healthful snacking include increased mental clarity, more energy, fewer cravings for junk food, and an overall feeling of well-being. As long as you do it correctly...

So, are your snacking habits healthy? Ask yourself the following questions to find out.

1. Do you really **need** *that snack?*

Are you snacking just for the sake of munching? Often snacks are chosen at inappropriate times or as a response to emotions like boredom or depression.

Break the habit: Pre-plan snack times. Choose 1 or 2 times each day when you find yourself going 5 hours or more between meals.

2. Is this a snack, or is it a treat?

A treat is a food that does not add value to your diet, while a snack provides valuable vitamins and minerals. See the difference between soda or a cupcake and Greek yogurt or nuts?

Break the habit: Before taking a bite, close your eyes and ask yourself which it is. If it's a snack, then go ahead and enjoy. If it's a treat, then put it back where it came from. You can do without it.

3. Are your snacks carb-overloaded?

Although whole-grain pretzels and fresh fruit sound like great snacks (and are most definitely healthy choices), they are more satisfying when combined with protein like Greek yogurt. Protein helps slow down the release of carbs so you do not get that familiar sugar rush, then crash and burn 20 minutes later.

Break the habit: Add protein like Greek yogurt or peanut butter to make snacks more satisfying and beneficial.

4. Are you choosing protein-only snacks?

On the flip side, going all-out on protein is not ideal either. It is important to add other foods, especially fruits and vegetables, to provide the fiber and antioxidants that are lacking in many diets. They also help you stay hydrated, contributing to your daily recommended dose of fluids.

Break the habit: Combine protein foods with fruits, whole-grain crackers, nuts, and vegetables for a well-balanced snack.

5. Are your portions in check?

Although you may be choosing the right foods to snack on, you may be consuming more calories than you think. Some foods may carry a "health halo" and have been hyped by the media, making you believe they are especially healthy, no matter the quantity. Although they may be a great addition to your eating plan, they may also be heavier on calories than you realize. Great examples are granola, peanut butter, whole-grain crackers, and avocados.

Break the habit: Review the serving size and amount of calories on the nutrition facts panel before munching, taking in somewhere between 125 and 250 calories with each snack.

6. Are you a mindless muncher?

Do you find yourself with a bottomless bag of almonds or dried fruit while watching television, texting, or surfing the Web? You may not be aware of what you are eating—or how much.

Break the habit: Pay attention to what you are snacking on and how much you are eating. Set out a portion rather than eating directly from the bag or container.

7. Are you relaxed and stress-free when you snack?

The environment in which you choose to snack matters. Munching hastily while running to your morning meeting is not very relaxing. You want to taste the food you are swallowing!

Break the habit: Choose a stress-free environment (like a park or a window with a view) and take 5 or 10 minutes to savor every bite. You will find snacks to be more satisfying, and reducing stress can help you achieve a healthier lifestyle.

So what's to eat? Select snack foods that will both satisfy and add value to your diet. You know what I'm going to say: Greek yogurt! Nonfat plain Greek yogurt has hunger-fighting protein, plus it provides calcium, magnesium, phosphorus, and potassium. Top it with fruit for extra fiber and antioxidants, or sprinkle it with 2 tablespoons of chopped almonds for a boost of healthy fat, fiber, vitamin E, riboflavin, magnesium, phosphorus, and copper. Here are ten easy-to-make Greek yogurt snack ideas for 250 calories or fewer.

Apples and Peanut Butter

¾ cup nonfat plain Greek yogurt
1 tablespoon natural peanut butter
½ teaspoon honey
1 small apple, sliced

Combine the Greek yogurt, peanut butter, and honey in a bowl. Dip apple slices into the yogurt mixture.

NUTRITION INFORMATION: Calories: 243; Total Fat: 8 grams; Protein: 16 grams; Total Carbohydrates: 31 grams; Fiber: 5 grams

Chocolate Delight

1 tablespoon unsweetened cocoa powder
1 tablespoon honey
¾ cup nonfat plain Greek yogurt
1 cup sliced strawberries

In a bowl, stir the cocoa powder and honey into the Greek yogurt. Top with the sliced strawberries.

NUTRITION INFORMATION: Calories: 224; Total Fat: 1 gram; Protein: 19 grams; Total Carbohydrates: 40 grams; Fiber: 4 grams

Lemon Meringue

3 vanilla wafers, crushed
¾ cup nonfat lemon Greek yogurt
2 tablespoons raw or dry-roasted chopped pecans

Place the crushed wafers in a small bowl. Top with the lemon Greek yogurt and sprinkle with the pecans.

NUTRITION INFORMATION: Calories: 235; Total Fat: 7 grams; Protein: 16 grams; Total Carbohydrates: 29 grams; Fiber: 1 gram

Tropical Frozen Yogurt

¼ cup diced fresh mango
¼ cup diced fresh pineapple
1 tablespoon agave syrup
¾ cup nonfat plain Greek yogurt

In a freezer-safe bowl, mix the mango, pineapple, and agave syrup into the Greek yogurt. Freeze for 2 to 3 hours before eating.

NUTRITION INFORMATION: Calories: 199; Total Fat: 0 grams; Protein: 18 grams; Total Carbohydrates: 34 grams; Fiber: 1 gram

Trail Mix

- ¾ cup nonfat plain Greek yogurt
- 1 tablespoon chopped cashews (dry-roasted, if desired)
- 1 tablespoon seedless raisins
- 2 teaspoons unsalted shelled sunflower seeds
- 3 dried apricots, diced

Place the Greek yogurt in a bowl and top with the cashews, raisins, sunflower seeds, and apricots.

NUTRITION INFORMATION: Calories: 245; Total Fat: 7 grams; Protein: 20 grams; Total Carbohydrates: 29 grams; Fiber: 3 grams

Peanut Butter and Jelly

- 1 tablespoon natural peanut butter
- 2 teaspoons jam, any flavor
- ¾ cup nonfat plain Greek yogurt

In a bowl, stir the peanut butter and jam into the Greek yogurt.

NUTRITION INFORMATION: Calories: 223; Total Fat: 8 grams; Protein: 21 grams; Total Carbohydrates: 19 grams; Fiber: 1 gram

Coconut-Almond Surprise

- 1 tablespoon sliced almonds
- 1 tablespoon unsweetened shredded coconut
- 2 teaspoons mini semisweet chocolate chips
- 1 teaspoon light brown sugar
- ¾ cup nonfat plain Greek yogurt

In a bowl, stir the almonds, coconut, chocolate chips, and brown sugar into the Greek yogurt.

NUTRITION INFORMATION: Calories: 225; Total Fat: 9 grams; Protein: 19 grams; Total Carbohydrates: 19 grams; Fiber: 1 gram

Berry-Tastic

- ¾ cup nonfat plain Greek yogurt
- ½ cup sliced fresh strawberries
- ¼ cup fresh blueberries
- ¼ cup fresh raspberries
- 1 tablespoon pure maple syrup

In a bowl, top the Greek yogurt with the strawberries, blueberries, and raspberries. Drizzle with the maple syrup.

NUTRITION INFORMATION: Calories: 206; Total Fat: 1 gram; Protein: 18 grams; Total Carbohydrates: 35 grams; Fiber: 5 grams

Key Lime Pie

- 1 tablespoon honey
- ½ teaspoon grated lime zest
- 1 tablespoon fresh lime juice
- ¾ cup nonfat plain Greek yogurt
- 3 graham crackers, crushed

In a bowl, stir the honey, lime zest, and lime juice, into the Greek yogurt. Top with the crushed graham crackers.

NUTRITION INFORMATION: Calories: 204; Total Fat: 1 gram; Protein: 18 grams; Total Carbohydrates: 34 grams; Fiber: 0 grams

Chocolate Grape Drizzle

- ½ cup nonfat vanilla Greek yogurt
- ½ cup seedless grapes, sliced
- 1 tablespoon chocolate syrup

Place the yogurt in a freezer-safe bowl. Top with the grapes and drizzle with the chocolate syrup. Place in the freezer for 2 to 3 hours.

NUTRITION INFORMATION: Calories: 164; Total Fat: 0 grams; Protein: 12 grams; Total Carbohydrates: 29 grams; Fiber: 1 gram

SHOPPING AND COOKING

Before beginning your adventure in the kitchen, getting to know the Greek yogurt aisle at the market can help you make smarter choices when shopping. Then, when you begin to cook with it, take the time to review its versatility in the kitchen.

At the Market

The selection of Greek yogurts at grocery stores is expanding rapidly, with more choices than ever. New flavors and snack packs are continually popping up. It can be overwhelming! Let's run down the basic varieties available.

Plain

- *Fat content:* full-fat, low-fat (2%), and nonfat (0%)
- *Sizes available:* Single-serving and tub sizes depend on the brand. The most common container sizes are 5.3 ounces, 6 ounces, and 7 ounces. Common tub sizes are 16 ounces, 17.6 ounces, 24 ounces, 32 ounces, and 35.3 ounces.

Blended Flavors

In these, the flavor has been blended throughout the yogurt.

- *Examples of flavors:* banana cream, blueberry, cherry, coconut, coffee, fig, honey, Key lime, lemon, mango, orange cream, orange vanilla, peach, pineapple, pomegranate, raspberry, strawberry, vanilla, vanilla chocolate chunk
- *Fat content:* Low-fat (2%) and nonfat (0%) are the most common. A handful of companies make full-fat blended flavors.
- *Sizes available:* Most blended flavors come in single-serving (5.3- or 6-ounce) containers. Only a couple of flavors, like vanilla and honey, come in tubs. The most common blended-flavor tub sizes are 16 ounces and 32 ounces.

Fruit on the Bottom

In these, the fruit is at the bottom of the container and you need to stir it in before eating.

- *Examples of flavors:* apple cinnamon, apricot, banana, blackberry, black cherry, blood orange, blueberry, mango, passion fruit, peach, pear, pineapple, pomegranate, raspberry, strawberry
- *Fat content:* low-fat (2%) and nonfat (0%)
- *Sizes available:* Only single-serving sizes are available (5.3- or 6-ounce containers).

Topping on the Side

Several companies have now developed Greek yogurt mix-ins and package them in a side compartment.

- *Examples of flavors:* almond coconut, banana with chocolate and nuts, blackberry and raspberry, blueberry chia, caramelized almonds, honey, honey apricot, honey banana, Key lime with graham crackers and white chocolate, mango, passion fruit, peach pistachio, pineapple, raspberry chocolate, strawberry, strawberry and honey oats, tropical fruit and granola, vanilla with honey oats and pecans
- *Fat content:* low-fat (2%) or nonfat (0%)
- *Sizes available:* Only single-serving sizes are available (5.3-ounce containers).

Minis

Smaller portions of flavored Greek yogurt are now available if you're looking for an even lower calorie snack.

- *Examples of flavors:* caramel pineapple, coffee and dark chocolate, fig with orange zest, honey ginger, mint chocolate chip, raspberry chocolate chip
- *Fat content:* low-fat (2%) or nonfat (0%)
- *Sizes available:* 3.5 ounces

Minis for Kids

The selections of Greek yogurt marketed to kids is also expanding rapidly. Here is what you will find:

- *Examples of flavors:* banana-honey, berry, blueberry, dragon fruit, mixed berry, orange vanilla, raspberry, strawberry, vanilla-chocolate
- *Fat content:* nonfat (0%)
- *Sizes available:* 3.5 ounces

Squeeze Tubes for Kids

- *Examples of flavors:* blueberry, cherry, dragon fruit, strawberry, strawberry-banana
- *Fat content:* nonfat (0%)
- *Sizes available:* 2.25 ounces

That's *a lot* of choices! So how do you pick without getting completely overwhelmed when you're at the grocery store? There are several things to keep in mind as you make your selection.

The Fat Content

Traditional yogurt is typically made with low-fat or nonfat milk to help keep fat and calories in check. Greek yogurt, however, can get a little tricky when it comes to fat. Full-fat varieties are packed with saturated fat, which has been shown to raise "bad" LDL cholesterol, thereby increasing the risk for heart disease. The USDA's Dietary Guidelines recommend choosing low-fat and nonfat dairy products as part of a healthy diet. Based on these recommendations, low-fat (2%) and nonfat (0%) varieties of Greek yogurt should be chosen on a regular basis. Keeping these guidelines in mind, I use only low-fat and nonfat varieties of both plain and flavored Greek yogurt in my recipes here. Luckily, you can find these varieties easily—opt for them whenever possible. If you do decide to indulge in full-fat Greek yogurt, I recommend doing so sparingly.

The Sugar Content

Another area of confusion is "added sugar" verses "natural sugar." One serving of plain nonfat Greek yogurt has around 6 grams of sugar. This sugar comes from lactose, the *natural* milk sugar found in Greek yogurt. Flavors like fruit or honey are considered *added* sugar and will cause the total grams of sugar to rise. But on the label, these numbers are combined and listed under "sugars." Be aware that for each additional 4 grams of sugar listed under "sugars," you are eating an equivalent of 1 teaspoon of added sugar. As a general rule of thumb, choose Greek yogurt varieties that list 20 grams of sugar or less on the nutrition label. Once it exceeds 3 teaspoons of added sugar, it kind of becomes dessert!

The Thickening Process

Another thing to keep in mind is how the Greek yogurt was thickened. As discussed earlier, some brands thicken their yogurt using traditional straining techniques, claiming that to be more natural. Others use thickening agents to achieve a dense and creamy texture and may label themselves "Greek-style" yogurt. There has been much debate within the Greek yogurt arena as to whether the use of added thickeners detracts from the authenticity of the product—and I believe it does! I would rather eat Greek yogurt that's been produced using the traditional straining processes than have extra unnecessary ingredients introduced. I always recommend a thorough review of the ingredient list to check if any thickening agents were added.

MAKING YOUR OWN GREEK YOGURT

Wondering what it takes to make your own Greek yogurt? If you see tubs of traditional yogurt on sale, buy a few and start straining! (Maybe you have some in your fridge right now, in which case you're ready to go!) It's actually pretty easy to strain a small batch—a good project for a rainy day or a fun experiment to set up with your kids. The goal is to take traditional yogurt and drain off the whey; the result is a thick, creamy, and slightly tangy Greek yogurt. Although the recipe at right starts with low-fat plain traditional yogurt, you can use nonfat plain or any blended flavored yogurt you like, such as vanilla. You may have seen this technique used to make yogurt cheese, which is another term for strained or Greek yogurt.

Homemade Low-Fat Greek Yogurt

Prep time: 10 minutes, plus 10 hours refrigeration *Cook time:* 0 minutes SERVES 2

2 cups low-fat plain traditional yogurt

SPECIAL EQUIPMENT:

1 medium-mesh strainer

1 medium bowl

3 cheesecloth squares

1 (16-ounce) can (content does not matter)

Place the mesh strainer over the bowl. Evenly layer the cheesecloth squares inside the strainer to line it. Place the yogurt in the center of the cheesecloth. Fold the sides of the cheesecloth over the yogurt, covering it tightly so the yogurt cannot ooze out under pressure.

Place the can on top of the cheesecloth to weight it down. Place the bowl in the refrigerator and allow the yogurt to drain for about 10 hours, until thick and creamy.

Remove from the refrigerator and serve, or place the strained yogurt in a covered container and store it in the refrigerator until the expiration date stamped on the original container.

SERVING SIZE: ½ cup

NUTRITION INFORMATION (PER SERVING): Calories: 120; Total Fat: 2 grams; Saturated Fat: 1 gram; Protein: 9 grams; Total Carbohydrates: 17 grams; Sugars: 15 grams; Fiber: 3 grams; Cholesterol: 7 milligrams; Sodium: 147 milligrams

In the Kitchen

Now that you've bought or made your own yogurt, it's time to get cooking! From breakfast to appetizers to salads to desserts, Greek yogurt can be used in a wide variety of dishes. This super-ingredient can be substituted for sour cream, cream cheese, mayonnaise, oil, buttermilk, heavy cream, and butter in both cooking and baking. It also adds texture to dips, sauces, and dressings. The Greek Yogurt Substitution Chart on the next page is a general outline of how to substitute nonfat or low-fat plain Greek yogurt in recipes.

GREEK YOGURT SUBSTITUTION CHART		
Food	*Substitute (nonfat or reduced-fat)*	*Recipes*
1 cup cream cheese	1 cup Greek yogurt	• Frosting
1 cup mayonnaise	1 cup Greek yogurt	• Baked potato topper • Tuna, egg, potato, and pasta salads • Dressings
1 cup sour cream	1 cup Greek yogurt	• Alongside Mexican fare • Dips • Cakes
1 cup heavy cream	1 cup Greek yogurt (add low-fat milk as needed to reach the desired consistency)	• Creamed spinach • Mashed potatoes • Cream-based sauces and soups (such as mushroom) • Cookies • Cupcakes • Pies • Biscuits • Panna cotta
1 cup butter (2 sticks)	¼ cup Greek yogurt plus ½ cup butter	• Cookies • Muffins • Brownies • Cheesecake • Frosting • Sauces (such as hollandaise) • Mashed potatoes
1 cup buttermilk	⅔ cup Greek yogurt plus ⅓ cup milk (reduced-fat or low-fat)	• Pancakes • Biscuits • Marinades • Ice cream • Salad dressings • Soups • Vegetable purees (such as mashed potatoes)
1 cup oil (such as canola or olive)	¾ cup Greek yogurt	• Breads • Muffins

Another fantastic way to use Greek yogurt is as a substitute for flavorful cheeses (like goat, ricotta, and mascarpone) and other ingredients (like pesto). Instead of eliminating these delicious flavors, substitute half the required quantity with nonfat plain Greek yogurt. One thing to note: Although you can swap cream cheese, mayonnaise, and sour cream for the exact amount of Greek yogurt, I like to combine the low-fat or light varieties (such as light mayonnaise or whipped cream cheese) with nonfat or low-fat Greek yogurt to maintain a touch of the intended flavor. As a general rule of thumb I use a 50:50 ratio, but the exact amount depends on the recipe. For example, when making a mayo-based dressing for my potato salad I substitute half the mayo with nonfat Greek yogurt and the other half with reduced-fat mayo. But I encourage you to have fun and experiment to find out what works best for your taste buds!

I've often been asked if Greek yogurt can be heated on the stovetop. The answer: absolutely! Greek yogurt can replace heavy cream and milk used to thicken stovetop recipes such as sauces. But without careful planning, the yogurt will curdle—that is, separate—when added to something hot. So how do you avoid ruining your dish-in-progress? One technique is tempering, or warming the Greek yogurt before adding it, which works well for sauces and soups: Place the needed amount of Greek yogurt in a small bowl. When it is time to add the yogurt to the dish, remove your pot or skillet from the heat or simply reduce the flame to low. Slowly stir several tablespoons of the sauce into the Greek yogurt in order to warm it up. Once the yogurt is slightly warmed, it can be stirred into the sauce without difficulty. You'll see this technique in the Beef Stroganoff on page 145 and the Chicken with Mushroom Sauce on page 137. Another safe way to avoid curdling is to remove the hot sauce or food from the heat and allow it to cool slightly before adding the Greek yogurt. We use this technique in the Penne Bolognese on page 149, the Spaghetti Squash Alfredo on page 167, and the Greek-Style Chicken with Olives, Tomatoes, and Feta on page 141. (These techniques can be used when cooking any soups and sauces that call for dairy. During cooking, the casein proteins tend to curdle when exposed to high heat, so when using milk or cream, it's also important to carefully control the amount of heat under the pot or skillet.)

Ten Surprising Uses

When I tell people that I use Greek yogurt to lighten Alfredo or bolognese sauce, they are quite surprised. But the versatility of this superstar ingredient goes far beyond that—all you need to do is to expand your imagination. Get inspired with these ten easy ways you can cook and bake with Greek yogurt.

1. **Hollandaise Sauce:** Combine a touch of butter, a few egg yolks, and nonfat plain Greek yogurt (plus a few flavorful low-calorie add-ins such as garlic, cayenne pepper, and Dijon mustard) to create a healthier version of this all-time favorite.

Try:

- *Eggs Benedict with Lighter Hollandaise (page 42)*
- *Roasted Asparagus with Hollandaise Sauce (page 177)*

2. **Deviled Eggs:** Put these sinister party favorites back on your "I can eat" list without the guilt. Greek yogurt can replace most (or all) of the mayonnaise, provide a creamy texture, and add protein and calcium.

Try: *Green Goddess Deviled Eggs (page 89)*

3. **Marinades:** Create your own flavorful marinade with Greek yogurt instead of oil. It helps keep fish, meat, and poultry tender and moist while also cutting down on the fat. Combine it with flavorful ingredients like fresh mint, garlic, scallions, Sriracha sauce, or reduced-sodium soy sauce.

Try:

- *Grilled Asian Shrimp Skewers with Dipping Sauce (page 129)*
- *Lamb Kebobs with Mint-Yogurt Sauce (page 143)*

4. **Dressings:** Replacing mayonnaise or buttermilk in creamy dressing is no surprise, but you can also use Greek yogurt to add body and flavor to thinner vinaigrette-type dressings.

Try:

- *Farro and Pea Shooters with Lime Dressing (page 87)*
- *Spinach Salad with Orange-Ginger Dressing (page 105)*
- *Arugula Salad with Pomegranate Dressing (page 103)*

5. **Guacamole:** Greek yogurt can help transform your everyday guacamole into a nutritional powerhouse. Besides adding creaminess and mouthfeel, it boosts the calcium and protein.

Try: *Mango Guacamole (page 79)*

6. **Spanakopita:** Welcome this usually sinful Greek spinach pie back into your healthy eating plan. Using Greek yogurt to replace part of the cheese and eggs will significantly cut calories, saturated fat, cholesterol, and sodium.

Try: *Spanakopita (page 96)*

7. **Cheese Pizza:** Replace part of the cheeses, such as ricotta or goat, with nonfat plain Greek yogurt. It cuts sodium and cholesterol along with fat and calories without compromising flavor.

Try:

- *White Cheese and Broccoli Rabe Pizza (page 164)*
- *White Margherita Pizza (page 155)*
- *Naan Bread Pizza with Olives, Mushrooms, and Peppers (page 169)*

8. **Cookies and Brownies:** Greek yogurt is a fabulous substitute for part of the butter in cookie and brownie recipes. As shown in the substitution chart, for each 1 cup of butter substitute ¼ cup of nonfat plain Greek yogurt plus ½ cup butter. This cuts down dramatically on both the calories and the artery-clogging fat.

Try:

- *Light and Dark Chocolate Brownies (page 220)*
- *Dirty Blondies (page 211)*

- *Coconut-Lemon Cookies (page 222)*
- *Double Chocolate Chip Cookies (page 197)*
- *Trail Mix Cookies (page 212)*

9. **Frosting:** Add the finishing touches to cakes and cupcakes without boatloads of butter and cream cheese. Greek yogurt helps maintain the delicious sweet flavor.

Try:

- *Layered Carrot Cake with Cream Cheese Frosting (page 206)*
- *Spiced Chocolate Cupcakes (page 216)*

10. **Popsicles:** Forgo the artificial coloring and overwhelming sweeteners. Make your own using fruits like mango, papaya, and banana—and combine with flavored or plain Greek yogurt.

Try:

- *Mojito Popsicles (page 225)*
- *Tropical Island Ice Pops (page 198)*

HOW TO USE THIS BOOK

By now you're probably dying to get cooking in your Greek yogurt kitchen! We're almost there. First, just a note on how to use this book. Not only do these recipes showcase the versatility of this superstar ingredient, but each fits into a healthy lifestyle. As such, the recipes are written slightly differently than a traditional recipe you're probably used to reading.

The Ingredients

I truly believe that healthy food should taste delicious. Why eat it if you don't enjoy it? That said, I also believe that foods should never be shunned from your healthy eating plan. You'll find ingredients like chocolate, butter, cheese, confectioners' sugar, and heavy cream sprinkled throughout my recipes. I use higher-fat and flavorful ingredients in very small portions, particularly with regard to cheeses. (I won't use fat-free cheese in cooking since I've never enjoyed the flavor and it doesn't melt well. I would rather use a small amount of full-fat cheese to season a dish or melt in a sandwich.) With all such ingredients, a little goes a long way! And you'll find fresh herbs, spices, vinegar, alcohol, low-sodium broth, fruit purees, and aromatic vegetables like onions and garlic throughout, as they add flavor for few calories.

What you *won't* see is artificial sweeteners. With early research linking large doses of certain artificial sweeteners with cancer, I'd rather just steer clear of them altogether. I use 100% fruit juice and regular jam or jelly because most lightened or sugar-free varieties use artificial sweeteners or sugar alcohols as replacements. To sweeten dishes, I use natural sweeteners that usually contain small doses of vitamins and minerals. My repertoire includes maple syrup, agave nectar, honey, and unsulphured molasses.

Milk appears in many recipes—it's another versatile ingredient I use in cooking and baking. You will find several types of milk at the store:

- *Whole milk:* made from 4% milk-fat milk
- *Reduced-fat milk:* also labeled as 2% milk
- *Low-fat milk:* also labeled as 1% milk
- *Nonfat milk:* also labeled as skim or fat-free milk

Nutrition Information and Serving Sizes

If you're trying to eat healthfully or are on a special diet, then you need the nutrition facts for anything you're eating! I've provided them for each recipe. They are listed per serving and include calories, total fat, saturated fat, protein, total carbohydrates, sugars, fiber, cholesterol, and sodium. As you read through each recipe—which I recommend doing before you start cooking, and before portioning it out to serve—be sure to review the serving size I list. If there is a sauce or dressing, I always specify *how much* should be used per serving.

Equipment

The recipes in this book use simple, wholesome ingredients and are easy to make. As a mom of three, I understand the importance of getting a healthy meal or snack on the table in a flash! Generally speaking, you won't need much more than pots, pans, and a blender or food processor. But several recipes do use special equipment. Here is a rundown of what you will need—you can purchase these items in advance so you have them on hand, though it's likely that you have a lot of them already.

- *Steamer basket:* White Cheese and Broccoli Rabe Pizza (page 164), Potato Salad with Parsnips and Edamame (page 186)
- *Double boiler:* Eggs Benedict with Lighter Hollandaise (page 42), Roasted Asparagus with Hollandaise Sauce (page 177)
- *Immersion blender:* Black Bean Soup with Lime-Zested Yogurt Cream (page 113), Egg Salad Tea Sandwiches (page 120)
- *Ramekins:* Crustless Mushroom Quiche (page 55), Lemon Panna Cotta with Orange-Thyme Sauce (page 199), Coconut Panna Cotta with Mango-Lime Coulis (page 214)
- *8-inch ceramic or glass pie dish:* Crustless Broccoli and Cheddar Quiche (page 45)
- *Shooter glasses:* Farro and Pea Shooters with Lime Dressing (page 87), Chocolate-Hazelnut Pudding Shooters (page 224)
- *Wooden skewers:* Grilled Asian Shrimp Skewers with Dipping Sauce (page 129), Lamb Kebobs with Mint-Yogurt Sauce (page 143)
- *Crème brûlée dishes:* Panna Cotta Brûlée (page 226)
- *Kitchen torch:* Panna Cotta Brûlée (page 226)
- *Trifle dish:* Pineapple-Coconut Trifle (page 202)
- *Standard popsicle molds:* Tropical Island Ice Pops (page 198), Mojito Popsicles (page 225)
- *Electric stand or hand mixer:* Vanilla-Lover Cupcakes (page 208)

Food Safety

I'm a huge advocate for food safety, and it's truly amazing how small habits in the kitchen can help prevent family members and friends from becoming sick. Some key practices to remember while cooking include:

- *Wash hands often:* I'm sure you've heard that you should sing the happy birthday song twice in order to make sure that your hands are thoroughly washed. But also make sure you're always stocked with soap and a means of drying your hands, such as single-use paper towels or cloth hand towels designated *only* for drying hands. Those kitchen towels that are used for every task from drying dishes to wiping countertops to taking hot food out of the oven get contaminated very quickly. They shouldn't be used for wiping your hands.

- *Avoid cross-contamination:* Many folks use the same knife and cutting board for raw meat, chicken, and fish, and then for fresh produce. Unknowingly, they're transferring bacteria from one food to another. Be sure to keep at least two cutting boards on hand—one for fruits and vegetables and the other for raw meats and fish. If you don't have two, then thoroughly wash the cutting board every time you begin to prepare a new food. And don't forget to wash the countertop, utensils, and your hands. Another common way to cross-contaminate is to use the same tongs or plate for both the raw and cooked food. Instead, have a separate plate and tongs or other serving utensil for the cooked food.

- *Marinate in the refrigerator:* When marinating meat, chicken, or fish, place it in a resealable container and then in the refrigerator. This will help minimize the growth of bad bacteria while your food is soaking up delicious flavors.

- *Check finished-cooking temperatures:* Although you may have been taught to check your chicken or other meat for color, or to see if the juices of poultry run clear, the best way to tell when your meat, poultry, or fish is safe to eat is by taking its temperature. If you don't have a digital food thermometer, I suggest you invest in one—you can easily find them for around $15. More expensive meat thermometers have built-in temperatures for different types of meats so you don't have to memorize every temperature. This can help to make your life easier.

When checking the temperature of a food, insert the thermometer in the thickest part, hold it for at least 15 seconds, and then take the reading. Here is a list of recommended finished-cooking temperatures:

- *Chicken and turkey (ground, pieces, or whole):* 165°F
- *Beef, pork, veal, and lamb (steaks and roasts):* 145°F
- *Beef, pork, veal, and lamb (ground):* 160°F
- *Fish:* 145°F or until fish is opaque and separates easily with a fork
- *Shrimp, lobster, crab:* Cook until flesh is pearly and opaque
- *Eggs:* Cook until white and yolk are firm

Phew! That was quite a lot of information! But you've made it through all the why and how. Now it's time for the fun part—the yum! I always love seeing finished dish photos. You can tweet them to me @tobyamidor! Now, let's get cooking...

CHAPTER 2

Breakfast

Cranberry Scones

I shy away from buying scones at my local French bakery because I know they're high in fat. Instead, I whip up a batch of these easy, light, and fluffy beauties. They pair perfectly with any hot morning toddy.

Prep time: 15 minutes *Cook time:* 15 minutes

MAKES 12 SCONES

- Cooking spray
- 1 cup unbleached all-purpose flour
- 1 cup whole wheat pastry flour
- 4 teaspoons baking powder
- ½ teaspoon salt
- ¼ teaspoon baking soda
- ½ cup granulated sugar
- 1 large egg
- 3 tablespoons canola oil
- 1 cup nonfat plain Greek yogurt
- ½ cup nonfat milk
- 1 teaspoon vanilla extract
- 1 cup dried unsweetened cranberries

Preheat the oven to 400°F. Coat two baking sheets with cooking spray and set them aside.

In a medium bowl, sift together the all-purpose flour, pastry flour, baking powder, salt, and baking soda.

In a separate medium bowl, whisk together the sugar, egg, canola oil, yogurt, milk, and vanilla extract.

Add the flour mixture to the yogurt mixture and begin to combine with a mixing spoon for just a few strokes. Then add the cranberries and mix carefully just until the dry ingredients are moistened, taking care not to overmix.

For each scone, drop a generous ⅓ cup of batter onto the prepared baking sheets, leaving about 2 inches of room all around. Bake until a toothpick inserted in the center of 1 or 2 scones comes out clean, about 15 minutes. Remove the baking sheets from the oven and allow to cool for 2 to 3 minutes. Then transfer the scones to a wire rack to cool for 10 minutes more.

SERVING SIZE: 1 scone

NUTRITION INFORMATION (PER SERVING): Calories: 188; Total Fat: 4 grams; Saturated Fat: 0 grams; Protein: 5 grams; Total Carbohydrates: 32 grams; Sugars: 16 grams; Fiber: 2 grams; Cholesterol: 16 milligrams; Sodium: 307 milligrams

Enjoy these scones with 1 tablespoon of Blueberry-Vanilla Jam (page 46).

Smoked Salmon Torte

Bagels and lox has been a longtime Sunday morning tradition in my home. But who needs the 400-plus calories from the bagel alone? This delicious torte has all the flavors I love (especially radishes and scallions!) for fewer than 250 calories per serving.

Prep time: 20 minutes *Cook time:* 0 minutes SERVES 4

- 2 (6½-inch) whole wheat pitas
- 1 cup nonfat plain Greek yogurt
- 4 ounces (⅔ cup) whipped cream cheese
- ½ English cucumber
- 1 medium tomato
- 4 red radishes
- 4 ounces smoked salmon
- 2 scallions

Using a serrated knife, carefully separate the pita pocket into two flat pita rounds. Store one flat pita round for another use and quarter the other three flat rounds, creating a total of 12 pieces.

In a small bowl, whisk together the yogurt and cream cheese; set aside. Slice the cucumber into ¼-inch-thick rounds. Halve the tomato and slice the halves into ¼-inch-thick slices. Slice the radishes into ¼-inch-thick rounds. Thinly slice the smoked salmon into strips.

In a deep round glass or ceramic serving dish, lay down 4 pita quarters to create 1 whole pita flat. Spread one-third of the yogurt mixture evenly over the pita quarters. Top with half the cucumbers, then half the tomatoes, and then half the radishes, distributing each evenly. Top with half of the smoked salmon in a flat layer. Repeat the layers, starting with 4 pita quarters. Top with the final 4 pita quarters and the remaining yogurt mixture. Chop the scallions, both whites and greens, and sprinkle over the top to garnish.

To serve, slice the torte into 4 wedges.

SERVING SIZE: 1 wedge (¼ of the torte)

NUTRITION INFORMATION (PER SERVING): Calories: 221; Total Fat: 10 grams; Saturated Fat: 5 grams; Protein: 15 grams; Total Carbohydrates: 20 grams; Sugars: 5 grams; Fiber: 3 grams; Cholesterol: 34 milligrams; Sodium: 498 milligrams

Lemon-Blueberry Stuffed French Toast

One morning I surprised my daughter with this stepped-up version of my challah French toast. She was enchanted with the tangy-sweet mixture of lemon yogurt and fresh blueberries—and I was pleased she was fueling up on a healthy breakfast.

Prep time: 15 minutes *Cook time:* 24 minutes SERVES 4

- Cooking spray
- 1 cup nonfat milk
- 4 large eggs
- 1 tablespoon vanilla extract
- ½ teaspoon ground cinnamon
- ½ loaf challah bread, preferably whole wheat
- 1¼ cups fresh or frozen blueberries (thawed if frozen)
- ¼ cup nonfat lemon Greek yogurt
- 1 tablespoon confectioners' sugar

Coat a large skillet with cooking spray. Heat it on the stove over medium-low heat.

In a medium bowl, whisk together the milk, eggs, vanilla extract, and cinnamon. Cut the challah into eight ½-inch-thick slices. Submerge half the slices in the egg mixture, being sure to moisten both sides. Then place the soaked slices on the heated skillet and cook until golden brown, about 7 minutes. Flip and cook on the other side until browned, about 5 minutes. Remove from the skillet and keep warm. Spray the skillet with cooking spray and repeat with the remaining 4 challah slices.

To make the filling, mash the blueberries and lemon yogurt together in a small bowl.

To assemble each stuffed French toast, place 1 piece of French toast on a plate. Spread ¼ cup of the lemon-blueberry mixture over the bread. Top with another piece of French toast, and slice in half. Just before serving, sprinkle the confectioners' sugar evenly over the stuffed French toast.

SERVING SIZE: 1 stuffed French toast

NUTRITION INFORMATION (PER SERVING): Calories: 379; Total Fat: 9 grams; Saturated Fat: 3 grams; Protein: 19 grams; Total Carbohydrates: 53 grams; Sugars: 19 grams; Fiber: 6 grams; Cholesterol: 232 milligrams; Sodium: 438 milligrams

Eggs Benedict with Lighter Hollandaise

Hollandaise sauce is typically made with a stick or two of butter to serve four people. The fat and calories can easily be slashed by substituting nonfat Greek yogurt for much of the butter, while still using a touch of butter to maintain the traditional flavor.

Prep time: 15 minutes *Cook time:* 24 minutes SERVES 4

- 2 teaspoons unseasoned rice vinegar
- 4 large eggs
- 2 whole wheat English muffins, split
- Cooking spray
- 4 slices turkey bacon (about ¼ pound)
- 2 tablespoons unsalted butter, at room temperature
- 2 cloves garlic, minced
- 12 medium asparagus spears, tough ends snapped off
- ½ cup nonfat plain Greek yogurt
- 2 large egg yolks
- 1 teaspoon fresh lemon juice
- ½ teaspoon Dijon mustard
- ⅛ teaspoon cayenne pepper
- ⅛ teaspoon kosher salt

To make a double boiler, fill a medium saucepan with 1 to 2 inches of water. Bring the water to a boil and then lower the heat to a simmer. Place a heatproof bowl on top of the pan; do not let the bottom of the bowl touch the simmering water. Place the ingredients—for hollandaise sauce, for example, or chocolate for melting—in the top bowl to heat gently.

In a large saucepan, bring 6 cups water to a boil over high heat. Add the vinegar and lower the heat until the water is no longer at a rolling boil. Crack an egg into a small cup, dish, or wineglass. Holding it near the surface of the water, gently slide the egg into the hot water. Repeat with the remaining eggs. Cover the saucepan and allow the eggs to cook for exactly 6 minutes. Remove each egg carefully with a slotted spoon and drain on a paper towel.

Toast the English muffins.

Coat a medium skillet with cooking spray and heat it over medium heat. Cook the bacon until cooked through, 2 to 3 minutes on each side. Place a slice of bacon on each toasted English muffin half.

In the same skillet, melt 1 tablespoon of the butter over medium heat. Add the garlic and cook until fragrant, about 30 seconds. Add the asparagus, cover the pan, and cook, tossing occasionally, until tender, about 8 minutes.

In a medium bowl, whisk the remaining 1 tablespoon butter with the yogurt, egg yolks, lemon juice, mustard, cayenne, and salt. Transfer the mixture to the top of a double boiler, set it over simmering water, and heat it, whisking continuously until the mixture thickens, about 5 minutes. Immediately remove from the heat.

To assemble the dish, place 3 asparagus spears over the bacon on each muffin half, and top with 1 poached egg and 2 tablespoons of the hollandaise sauce.

SERVING SIZE: 1 open sandwich half

NUTRITION INFORMATION (PER SERVING): Calories: 241; Total Fat: 13 grams; Saturated Fat: 6 grams; Protein: 15 grams; Total Carbohydrates: 16 grams; Sugars: 3 grams; Fiber: 3 grams; Cholesterol: 295 milligrams; Sodium: 301 milligrams

Chilled No-Cook Oatmeal with Strawberries and Dried Fruit

Take five minutes to prepare this oatmeal before you hit the sack, and by morning it will be ready to serve. No cooking, no mess, no fuss—my kind of breakfast!

Prep time: 5 minutes, plus 8 hours refrigeration *Cook time:* 0 minutes SERVES 4

- 8 medium fresh strawberries
- 2 cups old-fashioned rolled oats
- 2 cups nonfat plain Greek yogurt
- 2 tablespoons pure maple syrup
- 8 dried apricots, coarsely chopped
- ¼ cup seedless raisins
- ¼ teaspoon ground cinnamon
- 1 cup nonfat milk

Cut the strawberries into ¼-inch-thick slices. In a medium bowl, combine the oats, yogurt, strawberries, and maple syrup. Cover with plastic wrap and refrigerate for at least 8 hours or overnight.

Remove the oatmeal mixture from the refrigerator. Add the apricots, raisins, and cinnamon and stir to combine.

To serve, spoon ¾ cup of the oatmeal into each of four bowls and top each serving with ¼ cup milk. Serve cold or at room temperature.

SERVING SIZE: 1 bowl

NUTRITION INFORMATION (PER SERVING): Calories: 327; Total Fat: 3 grams; Saturated Fat: 1 gram; Protein: 19 grams; Total Carbohydrates: 58 grams; Sugars: 26 grams; Fiber: 6 grams; Cholesterol: 1 milligram; Sodium: 90 milligrams

Crustless Broccoli and Cheddar Quiche

I enjoy hosting Sunday morning brunch for friends where I can showcase my favorite recipes. This healthy quiche is always on my menu, and is a big hit with adults and kids alike.

Prep time: 12 minutes *Cook time:* 50 minutes SERVES 4

- Cooking spray
- 1 medium yellow onion
- 2 cloves garlic
- 1 pound broccoli florets
- 2 teaspoons grapeseed oil
- ¼ teaspoon salt
- ¼ teaspoon freshly ground black pepper
- 3 large eggs
- 2 large egg whites
- 1½ cups low-fat milk
- ½ cup low-fat plain Greek yogurt
- ⅛ teaspoon ground nutmeg
- 3 ounces shredded reduced-fat cheddar cheese (1 cup)

Preheat the oven to 425°F. Coat an 8-inch pie dish with cooking spray and set it aside.

Peel and chop the onion. Mince the garlic. Coarsely chop the broccoli florets.

In a medium skillet, heat the grapeseed oil over medium heat. When the oil is shimmering, add the onion and sauté until soft and translucent, 3 minutes. Add the garlic and cook until fragrant, 30 seconds. Add the broccoli and sauté, tossing occasionally, until it is bright green and tender, 5 minutes. Add ⅛ teaspoon each of the salt and pepper, and toss to combine. Remove the skillet from the heat and set it aside to cool slightly.

In a medium bowl, whisk together the eggs, egg whites, milk, yogurt, nutmeg, and the remaining ⅛ teaspoon salt and pepper until well combined.

To assemble the quiche, spread the broccoli mixture over the bottom of the prepared pie dish and sprinkle the cheddar cheese over the broccoli. Pour the egg mixture evenly over the top. Bake until the top is browned and a knife inserted about 1 inch from the edge comes out clean, 35 to 40 minutes. Serve warm.

SERVING SIZE: ¼ of the quiche

NUTRITION INFORMATION (PER SERVING): Calories: 244; Total Fat: 12 grams; Saturated Fat: 6 grams; Protein: 21 grams; Total Carbohydrates: 14 grams; Sugars: 8 grams; Fiber: 1 gram; Cholesterol: 160 milligrams; Sodium: 454 milligrams

Polish Breakfast Sandwich with Blueberry-Vanilla Jam

My dad is a sour-cream-and-jam type of guy—something he picked up from his Polish background. When I was growing up, we shared many sour cream and jam sandwiches, always on crispy bread. My three brothers put their own spin on it, scarfing down cream cheese and jelly sandwiches regularly. Once my guys tasted my homemade blueberry jam and Greek yogurt sandwiches, there was no looking back.

Prep time: 5 minutes *Cook time:* 35 minutes SERVES 4

- 3 cups fresh blueberries
- ½ cup granulated sugar
- 1 tablespoon fresh lemon juice
- ½ vanilla bean, sliced lengthwise, seeds scraped out and reserved, *or* ¼ teaspoon vanilla extract
- 4 whole wheat English muffins, split
- 1 cup nonfat plain Greek yogurt

To make the jam, combine the blueberries, sugar, lemon juice, and vanilla seeds (or vanilla extract) in a medium saucepan and toss to combine. Bring the mixture to a boil over medium heat. Then reduce the heat to medium-low and simmer, stirring occasionally, until thickened, about 35 minutes. Remove the pan from the heat and allow the mixture to cool to room temperature, about 10 minutes. Serve warm, or transfer to a container and store for up to 1 week in the refrigerator. (Makes 1 cup.)

To assemble the sandwiches, toast the English muffins. Spread 2 tablespoons of the yogurt on each English muffin half, and top with 1 tablespoon of the jam. Serve.

This Blueberry-Vanilla Jam and the Peach-Mango Chia Jam on page 56 can be prepared in advance and stored in an airtight container in the refrigerator for up to 1 week.

SERVING SIZE: 2 open-faced sandwiches

NUTRITION INFORMATION (PER SERVING): Calories: 190; Total Fat: 1 gram; Saturated Fat: 0 grams; Protein: 12 grams; Total Carbohydrates: 36 grams; Sugars: 13 grams; Fiber: 4 grams; Cholesterol: 0 milligrams; Sodium: 213 milligrams

Oat Pancakes with Berry-Yogurt Sauce

These pancakes boost whole grains and fiber, while the berry-yogurt topping replaces sugar-laden syrup and adds extra protein and antioxidants.

Prep time: 10 minutes *Cook time:* 15 minutes SERVES 6

- 1¼ cups fresh strawberries
- 2½ cups nonfat plain Greek yogurt
- 3 tablespoons honey
- ¾ cup fresh or frozen raspberries (thawed if frozen)
- 1 cup unbleached all-purpose flour
- ½ cup whole wheat pastry flour
- ½ cup old-fashioned rolled oats
- 3 tablespoons granulated sugar
- 1½ teaspoons baking powder
- ½ teaspoon baking soda
- ½ teaspoon salt
- 1 cup low-fat milk
- 4 teaspoons canola oil
- 2 large eggs
- ½ teaspoon vanilla extract
- Cooking spray

Cut the strawberries into ¼-inch-thick slices. In a small bowl, stir together 2 cups of the yogurt and the honey. Add the strawberries and raspberries, and stir gently to combine.

In a medium bowl, mix together the all-purpose flour, pastry flour, oats, sugar, baking powder, baking soda, and salt.

In a separate medium bowl, whisk together the milk, remaining ½ cup yogurt, canola oil, eggs, and vanilla extract. Pour the flour mixture into the milk-yogurt mixture and stir gently until combined, taking care not to overmix.

Coat a griddle or large skillet with cooking spray and heat it over medium heat. For each pancake, drop ¼ cup of the batter onto the pan, leaving about 2 inches between cakes. Cook until the tops are bubbly and the edges are set, about 2 minutes. Flip the pancakes over and cook for another 2 minutes, until golden and crisp. Transfer to a plate and cover with aluminum foil to keep warm. Repeat with the remaining batter.

To serve, place 2 pancakes on each plate and top with ½ cup of the berry-yogurt sauce.

SERVING SIZE: 2 pancakes plus ½ cup berry-yogurt sauce

NUTRITION INFORMATION (PER SERVING): Calories: 331; Total Fat: 6 grams; Saturated Fat: 1 gram; Protein: 17 grams; Total Carbohydrates: 53 grams; Sugars: 23 grams; Fiber: 4 grams; Cholesterol: 65 milligrams; Sodium: 506 milligrams

Banana-Walnut Muffins

In my house, these babies go like hotcakes (um, I mean muffins). To save time, I like to make a double batch and freeze half for later.

Prep time: 20 minutes *Bake time:* 15 minutes

MAKES 12 MUFFINS

- Cooking spray
- 2 ounces raw walnuts, coarsely chopped (⅔ cup)
- 3 tablespoons light brown sugar
- 1¼ teaspoons ground cinnamon
- 1½ cups unbleached all-purpose flour
- ½ cup whole wheat flour
- 2 teaspoons baking powder
- ½ teaspoon baking soda
- ½ teaspoon salt
- ⅛ teaspoon ground nutmeg
- 3 ripe bananas
- ½ cup nonfat plain Greek yogurt
- ⅓ cup granulated sugar
- 3 tablespoons canola oil
- 1 large egg, beaten
- 1 teaspoon vanilla extract

Preheat the oven to 400°F. Coat a standard 12-cup muffin tin with cooking spray and set it aside.

In a small bowl, combine the chopped walnuts, brown sugar, and ¼ teaspoon of the cinnamon.

In a medium bowl, sift together the all-purpose flour, whole wheat flour, baking powder, baking soda, salt, nutmeg, and remaining 1 teaspoon cinnamon.

In a separate medium bowl, mash the bananas, using a potato masher or a fork.

Overmixing batter makes cakes, cookies, and muffins tough instead of soft and chewy. As a rule of thumb, stop mixing the batter when no streaks of flour can be seen in the mixing bowl.

Whisk together the mashed bananas, yogurt, sugar, oil, egg, and vanilla extract.

Add the flour mixture to the yogurt mixture. Fold together gently, just until the dry ingredients are moistened, taking care not to overmix.

Spoon the batter into the prepared muffin cups. Top each cup with 2 teaspoons of the walnut mixture. Bake in the center of the oven until a toothpick inserted into the center of 1 or 2 muffins comes out clean, about 18 minutes.

Remove from the oven and allow to cool in the tin for 2 to 3 minutes. Then transfer the muffins to a wire rack to finish cooling for another 10 minutes.

SERVING SIZE: 1 muffin

NUTRITION INFORMATION (PER SERVING): Calories: 201; Total Fat: 7 grams; Saturated Fat: 1 gram; Protein: 5 grams; Total Carbohydrates: 32 grams; Sugars: 12 grams; Fiber: 2 grams; Cholesterol: 0 milligrams; Sodium: 239 milligrams

Blueberry-Bran Mini Muffins

When I am craving a yummy muffin, one or two of these flavorful minis will do the trick. Add a scrambled egg and a glass of low-fat milk and you've got a perfectly balanced breakfast.

Prep time: 20 minutes *Cook time:* 18 to 20 minutes MAKES 36 MINI MUFFINS

- Cooking spray
- 1½ cups unbleached all-purpose flour
- ¾ cup oat bran
- 1 teaspoon baking powder
- ½ teaspoon baking soda
- ⅛ teaspoon kosher salt
- ¼ cup (½ stick) unsalted butter, melted and cooled
- ¼ cup nonfat plain Greek yogurt
- ¼ cup apple butter
- ½ cup packed light brown sugar
- ¼ cup granulated sugar
- 2 large eggs
- 1 teaspoon vanilla extract
- 1 cup fresh or frozen blueberries (thawed if frozen)

Preheat the oven to 350°F. Coat 36 cups of two mini-muffin trays and set the trays aside.

In a medium bowl, mix together the flour, oat bran, baking powder, baking soda, and salt. Set aside.

In a large bowl, whisk together the melted butter, yogurt, and apple butter. Add the brown sugar and granulated sugar, and continue to whisk until the mixture is thoroughly combined and smooth. Add the eggs, one at a time, whisking until each is completely incorporated, and then whisk in the vanilla extract.

Slowly add the flour mixture to the yogurt mixture, stirring to combine. Gently fold the blueberries into the batter. Using a heaping tablespoon to measure, distribute the batter among the prepared mini muffin cups. Bake until the tops are golden brown and a toothpick inserted in the center of a muffin comes out clean, 18 to 20 minutes.

Remove from the oven and allow to cool in the tin for 2 to 3 minutes. Then transfer the muffins to a wire rack to finish cooling for another 10 minutes.

SERVING SIZE: 3 mini muffins

NUTRITION INFORMATION (PER SERVING): Calories: 182; Total Fat: 5 grams; Saturated Fat: 3 grams; Protein: 4 grams; Total Carbohydrates: 33 grams; Sugars: 17 grams; Fiber: 2 grams; Cholesterol: 41 milligrams; Sodium: 118 milligrams

Pumpkin Bread

When fall arrives each year, I love to bake this bread and fill my kitchen with the aromas of cinnamon, pumpkin, ginger, nutmeg, and cloves. Enjoy it with fresh fruit and a glass of milk for a quick and healthy breakfast.

Prep time: 15 minutes *Cook time:* 1 hour SERVES 10

- Cooking spray
- 1 cup unbleached all-purpose flour
- 1 cup whole wheat pastry flour
- ½ teaspoon ground cinnamon
- 1 teaspoon baking soda
- 1 teaspoon salt
- 1 teaspoon ground ginger
- ½ teaspoon ground nutmeg
- ¼ teaspoon ground cloves
- ¼ teaspoon baking powder
- ¾ cup canned pumpkin (I like Libby's)
- 3 tablespoons canola oil
- 2 large eggs, beaten
- 1 cup granulated sugar
- ¾ cup nonfat plain Greek yogurt
- ¼ teaspoon vanilla extract
- 3 ounces raw walnuts, coarsely chopped (about ¾ cup)

Preheat the oven to 350°F. Coat a 9 x 5-inch loaf pan with cooking spray and set it aside.

In a medium bowl, sift together the all-purpose flour, pastry flour, cinnamon, baking soda, salt, ginger, nutmeg, cloves, and baking powder.

In a separate medium bowl, whisk together the canned pumpkin, canola oil, eggs, sugar, yogurt, and vanilla extract. Add the chopped walnuts and stir to incorporate.

Add the flour mixture to the yogurt mixture and combine with as few strokes as possible, just until the dry ingredients are moistened, taking care not to overmix.

Spoon the batter into the prepared loaf pan and spread it into an even layer with a spatula. Bake until a toothpick inserted in the center comes out clean, about 1 hour.

Avoid canned pumpkin pie filling, which is loaded with sugar and preservatives. Instead, choose canned pumpkin purée made with 100% pure pumpkin.

Remove the pan from the oven and allow to cool for 5 minutes. Then transfer the bread to a wire rack to finish cooling for 10 to 15 minutes before slicing into 10 slices.

SERVING SIZE: 1 (¾-inch-thick) slice

NUTRITION INFORMATION (PER SERVING): Calories: 290; Total Fat: 11 grams; Saturated Fat: 1 gram; Protein: 7 grams; Total Carbohydrates: 42 grams; Sugars: 22 grams; Fiber: 3 grams; Cholesterol: 37 milligrams; Sodium: 397 milligrams

Mediterranean Stuffed Pitas

I spent many childhood summers in Israel. Every morning my mom would make us a chopped salad and sunny-side-up farm-fresh eggs. We enjoyed them with thick and creamy yogurt and warmed pita bread. I re-created that meal by packaging the ingredients together for this Mediterranean-inspired breakfast delight.

Prep time: 10 minutes *Cook time:* 5 minutes SERVES 4

- 1 English cucumber
- 1 red bell pepper
- 1 medium plum tomato
- 2 teaspoons fresh lemon juice
- 1 tablespoon extra-virgin olive oil
- ¼ teaspoon kosher salt
- ⅛ teaspoon freshly ground black pepper
- Cooking spray
- 4 large pasteurized eggs (see box on page 151)
- 2 (6½-inch) whole wheat pitas
- ½ cup nonfat plain Greek yogurt

Peel and chop the cucumber. Cut the bell pepper in half, discard the seeds, and chop. Chop the tomato. In a medium bowl, toss the chopped vegetables together. Add the lemon juice, olive oil, salt, and pepper and toss to coat evenly. Set aside.

Coat a medium skillet with cooking spray and heat it over medium heat. Crack an egg in a cup, and when the cooking spray is shimmering slightly, gently slide the egg into the skillet, taking care not to break the yolk. Cook until the white solidifies around the yolk, about 2 minutes. Then carefully flip it over and cook for 1 minute. Place the cooked egg on a large platter and cover with aluminum foil to keep warm. Repeat with the remaining eggs.

Using a serrated knife, cut the pitas in half to make pockets, and use your fingers to open them. Spoon 2 tablespoons yogurt, 1 over-easy egg, and ¼ cup of the salad into each pita. Serve with an additional ½ cup of the salad on the side.

In this recipe, the same amount of Parsley Hummus (page 76) or Babaganoush (77) can be substituted for the yogurt.

SERVING SIZE: ½ stuffed pita and ½ cup salad

NUTRITION INFORMATION (PER SERVING): Calories: 223; Total Fat: 9 grams; Saturated Fat: 2 grams; Protein: 13 grams; Total Carbohydrates: 23 grams; Sugars: 4 grams; Fiber: 4 grams; Cholesterol: 186 milligrams; Sodium: 398 milligrams

High-Protein Shake

Many folks dump spoonfuls of protein powder into their shakes, resulting in a grainy beverage. With the right ingredients, real food can do the trick. Greek yogurt not only gives this shake a protein punch, it also provides a creamy texture and delicious flavor.

Prep time: 5 minutes *Cook time:* 0 minutes SERVES 1

- ½ cup fresh or unsweetened frozen strawberries
- ½ cup fresh or unsweetened frozen mango
- ½ cup fresh or unsweetened frozen pineapple
- ½ cup nonfat milk or almond milk
- ½ cup nonfat plain Greek yogurt
- 2 tablespoons oat bran
- 2 pitted dried dates

Combine the fruit, milk, yogurt, oat bran, and dates in a blender and blend until smooth. Pour into a tall glass and serve.

SERVING SIZE: 12 fluid ounces

NUTRITION INFORMATION (PER SERVING): Calories: 373; Total Fat: 2 grams; Saturated Fat: 0 grams; Protein: 20 grams; Total Carbohydrates: 82 grams; Sugars: 65 grams; Fiber: 9 grams; Cholesterol: 2 milligrams; Sodium: 113 milligrams

Crustless Mushroom Quiche

Mushrooms are very low in calories (only about 20 per cup) and are brimming with nutrients like folate, thiamin, vitamin B_6, iron, and zinc. Mixed with the perfect protein—here, eggs—and served in individual ramekins, they make a delightfully good-for-you breakfast.

Prep time: 12 minutes *Cook time:* 40 minutes SERVES 4

- Cooking spray
- 1 shallot
- 4 ounces cremini mushrooms
- 4 ounces white mushrooms
- 2 teaspoons canola oil
- 1 teaspoon fresh thyme leaves
- ¼ teaspoon salt
- ¼ teaspoon freshly ground black pepper
- 3 large eggs
- 2 large egg whites
- 1½ cups low-fat milk
- ½ cup low-fat plain Greek yogurt
- ⅛ teaspoon ground nutmeg
- 2 ounces Fontina cheese, shredded (about ¾ cup)

Preheat the oven to 425°F. Coat four ramekins with cooking spray and set them aside.

Peel and finely chop the shallot. Chop the cremini mushrooms and white mushrooms. In a medium skillet, heat the canola oil over medium heat. When the oil is shimmering, add the shallot and sauté until soft and translucent, 2 minutes. Add the mushrooms and cook until softened, 5 minutes. Stir in the thyme and ⅛ teaspoon each of the salt and pepper. Cook for 1 minute more. Remove the skillet from the heat and set it aside to cool slightly.

In a medium bowl, whisk together the eggs, egg whites, milk, yogurt, nutmeg, and remaining ⅛ teaspoon salt and pepper.

Ladle ¼ cup of the mushroom mixture into each ramekin. Sprinkle each with 3 tablespoons of the cheese, and then top with ¾ cup of the egg mixture. Bake until a knife inserted in the center comes out clean and the tops are browned, 30 minutes. Serve warm.

SERVING SIZE: 1 quiche

NUTRITION INFORMATION (PER SERVING): Calories: 223; Total Fat: 12 grams; Saturated Fat: 5 grams; Protein: 18 grams; Total Carbohydrates: 11 grams; Sugars: 8 grams; Fiber: 1 gram; Cholesterol: 163 milligrams; Sodium: 400 milligrams

Egg yolks contain the antioxidant lutein, which has been shown to promote healthy skin and eyes. Research has found that lutein from eggs is better absorbed than lutein from other foods.

Greek Yogurt with Peach-Mango Chia Jam

Chia seeds thicken and swell by absorbing the liquid in anything they're incorporated into—like jam and pudding. If you're not familiar with cooking them, this easy recipe is the perfect place to get started.

Prep time: 5 minutes *Cook time:* 15 minutes SERVES 4

- 1 cup fresh or unsweetened frozen peach slices
- 1 cup fresh or unsweetened frozen mango slices
- 1 tablespoon chia seeds
- 2 cups nonfat plain Greek yogurt

Place the peach and mango slices in a small saucepan over medium heat. Cook, stirring often, until soft, about 12 minutes. Then use a potato masher or a fork to mash the fruit in the pan. Reduce the heat to low and add the chia seeds. Stir to combine. Cook until the mixture thickens, about 3 minutes. Remove the pan from the heat and allow to cool for 5 minutes.

Carefully transfer the hot peach-mango mixture to a blender and puree until smooth.

To serve, place ½ cup yogurt into each of four cups or bowls. Stir in 2 tablespoons of the jam.

SERVING SIZE: ½ cup yogurt and 2 tablespoons jam

NUTRITION INFORMATION (PER SERVING): Calories: 115; Total Fat: 1 gram; Saturated Fat: 0 grams; Protein: 17 grams; Total Carbohydrates: 12 grams; Sugars: 11 grams; Fiber: 1 gram; Cholesterol: 0 milligrams; Sodium: 68 milligrams

Morning Tropical Fruit and Almond Crunch

This colorful combination of kiwi, strawberries, and mango is a delicious and antioxidant-packed way to start your morning. Plus, the fiber from the fruit and almonds, along with the protein from the Greek yogurt, will help curb your hunger throughout the morning.

Prep time: 15 minutes, plus 30 minutes refrigeration *Cook time:* 5 minutes SERVES 4

- ½ cup raw or dry-roasted unsalted sliced almonds
- 2 kiwis
- 1 mango
- 6 medium fresh strawberries
- 2 tablespoons 100% orange juice
- 1 tablespoon granulated sugar
- 1 teaspoon vanilla extract
- 2 cups nonfat plain Greek yogurt
- 4 teaspoons pure maple syrup

If you're using raw almonds, preheat the oven to 350°F.

Spread the almonds in an even layer on a baking sheet and toast in the oven until fragrant and slightly browned, about 5 minutes. Remove the baking sheet from the oven and set it aside to cool. (If your almonds are already dry-roasted, skip this step.)

Peel and dice the kiwis and mango. Slice the strawberries. In a medium bowl, whisk together the orange juice, sugar, and vanilla extract. Add the fruit and toss gently until evenly coated. Cover and refrigerate for 30 minutes to allow the flavors to combine.

To assemble, place ½ cup of the yogurt in each of four bowls. Top each with a heaping ½ cup of the fruit salad, 2 tablespoons of the almonds, and 1 teaspoon of the maple syrup.

SERVING SIZE: 1 bowl

NUTRITION INFORMATION (PER SERVING): Calories: 213; Total Fat: 6 grams; Saturated Fat: 0 grams; Protein: 15 grams; Total Carbohydrates: 28 grams; Sugars: 21 grams; Fiber: 4 grams; Cholesterol: 0 milligrams; Sodium: 49 milligrams

Looking to save time? Prepare the fruit salad the night before and store it in an airtight container in the refrigerator.

Zucchini Bread

Every summer I'm excited when zucchini season hits so I can whip up this easy bread. Half the fat is replaced with just ¼ cup of Greek yogurt.

Prep time: 25 minutes *Cook time:* 45 minutes SERVES 8

- Cooking spray
- 1 cup whole wheat pastry flour
- 1 teaspoon ground cinnamon
- ½ teaspoon baking powder
- ¼ teaspoon baking soda
- ¼ cup (½ stick) unsalted butter, melted and cooled
- ¼ cup nonfat plain Greek yogurt
- ½ cup packed light brown sugar
- 1 teaspoon vanilla extract
- 2 large eggs
- 1 medium zucchini, shredded
- 2 medium carrots, peeled and shredded

Preheat the oven to 350°F. Coat an 8-inch loaf pan with cooking spray and set it aside.

In a medium bowl, sift together the flour, cinnamon, baking powder, and baking soda.

In a large bowl, whisk together the melted butter and the yogurt. Add the brown sugar and vanilla extract, and whisk until the mixture is uniform and smooth. Add the eggs, one at a time, continuing to whisk.

Gradually stir the flour mixture into the yogurt mixture. When completely combined, gently fold in the zucchini and carrots until evenly distributed.

Pour the mixture into the prepared pan, spreading it into an even layer with a spatula. Bake until the top is golden brown and a toothpick inserted in the center comes out clean, about 45 minutes. Remove the pan from the oven and allow to cool for 5 minutes. Then transfer the bread to a wire rack and let it cool for 10 to 15 minutes before cutting it into 1-inch-thick slices.

SERVING SIZE: 1 (1-inch-thick) slice

NUTRITION INFORMATION (PER SERVING): Calories: 240; Total Fat: 12 grams; Saturated Fat: 8 grams; Protein: 4 grams; Total Carbohydrates: 27 grams; Sugars: 15 grams; Fiber: 2 grams; Cholesterol: 77 milligrams; Sodium: 90 milligrams

Peach Oatie Smoothie

Smoothies are a fun way to add oats to your morning without turning on the stove. In this recipe, soaking the oats will hydrate them, making them easy to soften and incorporate into a beverage.

Prep time: 15 minutes, plus 30 minutes freezing *Cook time:* 0 minutes SERVES 1

- 1/4 cup nonfat milk
- 1 tablespoon old-fashioned rolled oats
- 1 1/2 cups unsweetened frozen peach slices (see box on page 66)
- 1/2 cup peach nectar (I like Bionaturae)
- 1/4 cup nonfat vanilla Greek yogurt
- 1/8 teaspoon ground cinnamon

Place a 12-ounce glass in the freezer and allow it to chill for at least 30 minutes.

Place the milk and oats in a blender jar and stir with a spoon to combine. Allow the oats to hydrate for at least 10 minutes or up to 30 minutes.

Add the peach slices, peach nectar, yogurt, and cinnamon to the oat mixture in the blender. Cover and blend until smooth. Pour into the chilled glass and serve immediately.

SERVING SIZE: 12 fluid ounces

NUTRITION INFORMATION (PER SERVING): Calories: 227; Total Fat: 0 grams; Saturated Fat: 0 grams; Protein: 9 grams; Total Carbohydrates: 49 grams; Sugars: 41 grams; Fiber: 4 grams; Cholesterol: 1 milligram; Sodium: 58 milligrams

Choose a peach nectar that does not contain high-fructose corn syrup. Read the ingredient list carefully.

Light soy milk, almond milk, or unsweetened coconut milk can be used in place of nonfat milk if desired. If you are lactose intolerant, you can also try lactose-free milk, such as Lactaid.

Whole-Grain Banana–Chocolate Chip Pancakes

Weekend mornings are the perfect time to enjoy a relaxing breakfast and catch up with my husband and our kids. I feel good about whipping up these better-for-you pancakes for my family, and they have become one of the most requested breakfasts in our home.

Prep time: 12 minutes *Cook time:* 10 minutes SERVES 8

- 1 cup unbleached all-purpose flour
- 1 cup whole wheat pastry flour
- ¼ cup granulated sugar
- 2 teaspoons baking powder
- ½ teaspoon salt
- 2 large eggs
- ¼ cup canola oil
- 1 cup nonfat milk
- 1 cup nonfat plain Greek yogurt
- ⅓ cup dark chocolate chips
- 2 medium bananas
- Cooking spray
- ½ cup pure maple syrup

In a medium bowl, sift together the all-purpose flour, pastry flour, sugar, baking powder, and salt. Set aside.

In a large bowl, whisk together the eggs, canola oil, and milk. Add the yogurt and whisk to combine.

Add the dry mixture to the yogurt mixture. Stir to combine, taking care not to overmix. Fold in the chocolate chips.

Cut the bananas into ¼-inch-thick rounds.

Spray a large skillet with cooking spray and heat it over medium heat. For each pancake, drop a heaping ¼ cup of the batter into the skillet, and sprinkle 2 or 3 banana slices on top. Repeat, leaving about 2 inches between pancakes. Cook until the tops are bubbly and the edges are set, 2 to 3 minutes. Flip the pancakes over and cook for another 2 minutes, until golden and crisp. Transfer to a plate and cover with aluminum foil to keep warm. Repeat with the remaining batter and bananas.

Heard that dark chocolate is healthy? It is! That's because dark chocolate contains more cocoa, which is where you'll find all the good-for-you nutrients—including the antioxidant theobromine, *found to help reduce inflammation and lower blood pressure.*

To serve, place 2 pancakes on each of eight plates and drizzle 1 tablespoon of maple syrup over each stack.

SERVING SIZE: 2 pancakes plus 1 tablespoon syrup

NUTRITION INFORMATION (PER SERVING): Calories: 359; Total Fat: 10 grams; Saturated Fat: 2 grams; Protein: 9 grams; Total Carbohydrates: 58 grams; Sugars: 28 grams; Fiber: 3 grams; Cholesterol: 3 milligrams; Sodium: 315 milligrams

Southwestern Egg Wrap

When I was a little girl, my family lived in El Paso, Texas, for a short while. Although Texas was a big change for a Brooklyn girl, I quickly grew accustomed to the mouthwatering Tex-Mex fare. Now, back in New York, I have learned to lighten up this traditionally high-calorie cuisine by bulking up on flavorful ingredients like cilantro, tomatoes, onion, jalapeño, and chili powder and swapping out sour cream for nonfat Greek yogurt.

Prep time: 15 minutes *Cook time:* 15 minutes SERVES 6

- 2 teaspoons olive oil
- 1 small yellow onion, peeled and chopped
- 1 jalapeño pepper, halved, seeded, and cut into ⅛-inch dice
- 1 (15-ounce) can no-salt-added black beans
- ½ teaspoon chili powder
- ¼ teaspoon ground cumin
- ¼ teaspoon garlic powder
- ¼ teaspoon kosher salt
- ¼ teaspoon freshly ground black pepper
- Cooking spray
- 6 large eggs
- 6 tablespoons reduced-fat sour cream
- 6 tablespoons nonfat plain Greek yogurt
- ¼ cup chopped fresh cilantro leaves
- 2 large plum tomatoes, diced
- 1 tablespoon fresh lime juice
- 6 (8-inch) 100% whole wheat tortillas
- 2 ounces reduced-fat Monterey Jack cheese, shredded (¾ cup)

In a medium skillet, heat the olive oil over medium heat. When the oil is shimmering, add the onion and jalapeño, and cook until the onions are translucent, about 2 minutes.

Drain the black beans in a colander or strainer, and rinse them. Add the beans to the skillet and cook until the mixture is heated through, 2 minutes. Add the chili powder, cumin, garlic powder, and ⅛ teaspoon each of the salt and pepper. Cook, stirring occasionally, until the flavors combine, about 5 minutes. Transfer the bean mixture to a bowl and cover with aluminum foil to keep warm.

Wipe out the skillet with a paper towel. Coat the skillet with cooking spray and return it to medium heat. In a medium bowl, whisk the eggs with the remaining ⅛ teaspoon salt and pepper. Add the eggs to the heated skillet. Using a spatula, fold and invert the eggs until large, soft curds form, 3 to 4 minutes. Remove from the heat and set aside.

In a small bowl, stir together the sour cream, yogurt, and cilantro. In another small bowl, toss the tomatoes with the lime juice. Set both aside.

To assemble the wraps, place one tortilla on each of six plates. Top each tortilla with one sixth of the scrambled eggs, ⅓ cup of the bean mixture, 2 tablespoons of the yogurt mixture, 2 tablespoons of the tomatoes, and 2 tablespoons of the cheese. Roll up each wrap and serve immediately.

SERVING SIZE: 1 wrap

NUTRITION INFORMATION (PER SERVING): Calories: 340; Total Fat: 15 grams; Saturated Fat: 5 grams; Protein: 19 grams; Total Carbohydrates: 35 grams; Sugars: 4 grams; Fiber: 8 grams; Cholesterol: 200 milligrams; Sodium: 600 milligrams

Green Spa Shake

I cherish my visits to the spa and wanted to re-create that tranquil feeling in my own home. The combination of lemon and basil reminds me of the flavored water and snacks served in the quiet room at the spa.

Prep time: 5 minutes *Cook time:* 0 minutes

SERVES 1

- 4 fresh basil leaves
- ½ medium avocado
- ½ cup nonfat plain Greek yogurt
- ½ cup nonfat milk, light soy milk, or rice milk
- 2 tablespoons fresh lemon juice (from about 1 small lemon)
- 4 teaspoons honey

Coarsely chop the basil leaves. Combine the basil, avocado pulp, yogurt, milk, lemon juice, and honey in a blender, and blend until smooth. Pour into a glass and serve.

SERVING SIZE: 8 fluid ounces

NUTRITION INFORMATION (PER SERVING): Calories: 372; Total Fat: 15 grams; Saturated Fat: 3 grams; Protein: 19 grams; Total Carbohydrates: 47 grams; Sugars: 37 grams; Fiber: 9 grams; Cholesterol: 2 milligrams; Sodium: 100 milligrams

To keep recipes as wholesome as possible, I recommend using fresh lemon juice over the bottled varieties, which are packed with preservatives.

All-American Parfait

The addition of toasted coconut, crunchy almonds, and sweet and tart orange-flavored strawberries takes this recipe up a notch.

Prep time: 15 minutes *Cook time:* 8 minutes

SERVES 4

- ¾ cup unsweetened shredded coconut
- 1½ ounces raw or dry-roasted unsalted almonds, chopped (¼ cup)
- ¼ cup 100% orange juice
- 1 teaspoon grated orange zest
- 3 cups fresh or frozen sliced strawberries (thawed if frozen)
- 2 cups nonfat honey Greek yogurt
- 2 cups fresh or frozen blueberries (thawed if frozen)

Preheat the oven to 350°F.

Spread the shredded coconut on a baking sheet and toast in the oven until lightly browned, 3 to 4 minutes. Remove the baking sheet from the oven and set it aside to cool.

If your chopped almonds are raw, toast them in a small sauté pan over medium-low heat until fragrant and lightly browned, 1 to 2 minutes. Set aside. (Skip this step if they're dry-roasted.)

In a medium bowl, whisk together the orange juice and zest. Add the strawberries and toss to coat evenly. Set aside to marinate for at least 15 minutes or as long as 1 hour.

In a separate medium bowl, combine the toasted coconut and the yogurt.

To assemble the parfaits, layer the bottom of each of four glasses with ⅓ cup of the strawberries, then 3 heaping tablespoons of the yogurt-coconut mixture, followed by ¼ cup of the blueberries. Repeat the layers once more, and then sprinkle each parfait with 1 tablespoon of the toasted almonds.

SERVING SIZE: 1 parfait

NUTRITION INFORMATION (PER SERVING): Calories: 292; Total Fat: 11 grams; Saturated Fat: 5 grams; Protein: 14 grams; Total Carbohydrates: 39 grams; Sugars: 28 grams; Fiber: 7 grams; Cholesterol: 0 milligrams; Sodium: 45 milligrams

Berry Greek Smoothie

There is no skipping breakfast in my house. My mother instilled this healthy habit in me when I was growing up, and I have done the same with my kids. But some days I'm in a rush getting myself plus three kids out the door. This smoothie always does the trick—it's super quick and easy to make.

Prep time: 5 minutes *Cook time:* 0 minutes SERVES 1

- 1½ cups unsweetened frozen strawberries
- ½ cup nonfat plain Greek yogurt
- ½ cup 100% cranberry juice
- 2 teaspoons honey

Combine the strawberries, yogurt, cranberry juice, and honey in a blender and blend until smooth. Pour into a tall glass and serve.

SERVING SIZE: 12 fluid ounces

NUTRITION INFORMATION (PER SERVING): Calories: 211; Total Fat: 0 grams; Saturated Fat: 0 grams; Protein: 0 grams; Total Carbohydrates: 43 grams; Sugars: 37 grams; Fiber: 3 grams; Cholesterol: 0 milligrams; Sodium: 54 milligrams

I prefer using frozen fruit in smoothies to enhance the flavor and add an icy texture. If you're using fresh fruit, place it in the freezer at least 1 day in advance. Most fruit can be frozen for about 3 months.

Whole-Grain Banana–Chocolate Chip Pancakes (page 60)

Eggs Benedict with Lighter Hollandaise (page 42)

Fig and Walnut Parfait (page 70)

Baked Artichoke Dip with
Fontina Cheese (page 75)

Lemon-Blueberry Stuffed French Toast (page 41)

Asian Lettuce Cups with
Broccoli Slaw and Chicken (page 83)

Herbed Goat Cheese and Red Pepper Crostini (page 88)

Green Goddess Deviled Eggs (page 89)

Sesame-Ginger Salmon Croquettes
with Sriracha Cream (page 92)

Tangy Buffalo-Style Salad with Chicken (page 108)

Soba Noodle Salad with Peanut Sauce (page 110)

Avocado Soup with Pineapple Salsa (page 118)

Salad Parfait (page 102)

Chilled Tomato-Herb Soup (page 117)

Lighter Lobster Rolls (page 121)

Caprese Panini (page 122)

Pineapple-Orange Yogurt Parfait

Brighten your morning with sunshine-yellow pineapple layered with tart Greek yogurt and topped with toasted pumpkin seeds. It's a tasty way to provide the nutritional goodness your body needs to start your day off right.

Prep time: 5 minutes *Cook time:* 2 minutes SERVES 4

- ½ cup unsalted shelled pumpkin seeds
- 2 cups nonfat vanilla Greek yogurt
- 2 cups nonfat plain Greek yogurt
- 2 tablespoons honey
- ⅛ teaspoon ground nutmeg
- 2 cups canned crushed pineapple in juice
- 2 teaspoons grated orange zest
- 4 fresh mint leaves

In a small sauté pan set over medium-low heat, toast the pumpkin seeds until fragrant and lightly browned, about 2 minutes. Remove the pan from the heat and set it aside to cool.

In a small bowl, stir together both yogurts, the honey, and the nutmeg.

In a separate small bowl, combine the pineapple and the orange zest.

To assemble the parfaits, layer the bottom of each of four glasses with ½ cup of the yogurt mixture. Top each with ¼ cup of the pineapple mixture and 1 tablespoon of the pumpkin seeds. Repeat the layers once more, and garnish each parfait with a mint leaf.

SERVING SIZE: 1 parfait

NUTRITION INFORMATION (PER SERVING): Calories: 335; Total Fat: 8 grams; Saturated Fat: 1 gram; Protein: 28 grams; Total Carbohydrates: 41 grams; Sugars: 36 grams; Fiber: 2 grams; Cholesterol: 0 milligrams; Sodium: 102 milligrams

To cut back on sugar, skip canned fruits packed in syrup. Instead, choose those packed in their own juices.

Sun-Kissed Smoothie

One of my favorite places to vacation is the Caribbean Islands. I wake up each morning and order a platter filled with mango, papaya, and other sun-kissed fruit. When I miss my delicious vacations, I make this smoothie as a sweet reminder.

Prep time: 5 minutes *Cook time:* 0 minutes SERVES 1

- ½ cup fresh or unsweetened frozen mango chunks
- ½ cup fresh or unsweetened frozen pineapple chunks
- ½ cup fresh or unsweetened frozen diced papaya
- ½ cup nonfat plain Greek yogurt
- ½ cup unsweetened coconut milk
- 1 teaspoon blue agave (I like Wholesome Sweeteners)

Combine the fruit, yogurt, coconut milk, and agave in a blender and blend until smooth. Pour into a tall glass and serve.

SERVING SIZE: 12 fluid ounces

NUTRITION INFORMATION (PER SERVING): Calories: 233; Total Fat: 3 grams; Saturated Fat: 3 grams; Protein: 12 grams; Total Carbohydrates: 41 grams; Sugars: 37 grams; Fiber: 4 grams; Cholesterol: 0 milligrams; Sodium: 127 milligrams

Elvis Smoothie

Elvis loved his peanut butter and banana sandwiches—the inspiration for this smoothie. Although he reportedly added bacon, we'll be going in a healthier direction with raspberries instead.

Prep time: 5 minutes *Cook time:* 0 minutes SERVES 1

1 ripe banana
½ cup unsweetened frozen raspberries
½ cup nonfat milk or light soy milk
1 (5.3-ounce) container nonfat raspberry Greek yogurt
1 tablespoon natural creamy peanut butter

Combine the banana, raspberries, milk, yogurt, and peanut butter in a blender and blend until smooth. Pour into a tall glass and serve.

SERVING SIZE: 12 fluid ounces

NUTRITION INFORMATION (PER SERVING): Calories: 382; Total Fat: 9 grams; Saturated Fat: 2 grams; Protein: 24 grams; Total Carbohydrates: 59 grams; Sugars: 34 grams; Fiber: 6 grams; Cholesterol: 2 milligrams; Sodium: 229 milligrams

When shopping for peanut butter, look for a natural version made with just two ingredients: peanuts and salt. Although reduced-fat peanut butter may seem to be the healthier choice, many are high in sugar and preservatives. I like Skippy or Trader Joe's.

Fig and Walnut Parfait

This parfait has become one of my absolute favorite breakfasts! Pieces of sweet dried figs mixed together with crunchy omega-3-rich walnuts just hit the right spot first thing in the morning.

Prep time: 15 minutes *Cook time:* 8 minutes SERVES 4

- 2 ounces raw walnuts, chopped (about ½ cup)
- 4 ounces (8 to 10 whole) dried Black Mission figs, chopped
- 2 tablespoons pure maple syrup
- 2 cups nonfat honey Greek yogurt

In a small saucepan over medium-low heat, toast the walnuts, tossing them every 30 seconds, until fragrant and lightly browned, about 5 minutes. Add the figs to the pan and cook until the mixture is warmed through, about 1 minute. Add the maple syrup and stir to coat evenly. Allow to cook, stirring continuously, until all the liquid has evaporated, about 2 minutes. Remove the pan from the heat and set it aside to cool.

To make the parfaits, layer each of four glasses with ¼ cup of the yogurt, then 2 tablespoons of the fig-walnut mixture, and then an additional ¼ cup of the yogurt. Top with an additional 3 tablespoons of the fig-walnut mixture. Serve immediately.

SERVING SIZE: 1 parfait

NUTRITION INFORMATION (PER SERVING): Calories: 290; Total Fat: 9 grams; Saturated Fat: 1 gram; Protein: 13 grams; Total Carbohydrates: 43 grams; Sugars: 35 grams; Fiber: 4 grams; Cholesterol: 8 milligrams; Sodium: 44 milligrams

CHAPTER 3

Snacks and Appetizers

Kale Dip

Move over spinach dip—kale is the new leafy green in town! Blend this popular member of the cabbage family with creamy Greek yogurt and light mayo for the perfect combination. I serve it with raw vegetables or pita chips when I'm hosting ladies' mah-jongg night—and it's always big hit!

Prep time: 12 minutes *Cook time:* 1 minute SERVES 8

- 1 bunch fresh kale (about 12 ounces)
- 1 clove garlic
- 1 cup nonfat plain Greek yogurt
- 2 tablespoons light mayonnaise
- ½ teaspoon fresh lemon juice
- ½ teaspoon kosher salt
- ¼ teaspoon freshly ground black pepper

Fill a large pot with water and bring it to a boil over high heat. Meanwhile, wash and chop the kale.

Add the kale to the boiling water and cook until it is bright green, about 1 minute. Drain it well and set aside to cool completely, about 5 minutes.

Mince the garlic. Place the kale, yogurt, mayonnaise, garlic, lemon juice, salt, and pepper in a blender or food processor. Blend until smooth, about 30 seconds.

Serve immediately, or cover and store in the refrigerator for up to 3 days.

SERVING SIZE: ¼ cup

NUTRITION INFORMATION (PER SERVING): Calories: 49; Total Fat: 2 grams; Saturated Fat: 0 grams; Protein: 4 grams; Total Carbohydrates: 6 grams; Sugars: 1 gram; Fiber: 1 gram; Cholesterol: 1 milligram; Sodium: 202 milligrams

White Bean Dip

Last-minute guests can never get over the fact that I always have food ready. My secret is to keep several cans of cannellini beans in my pantry so I am always prepared. This delicious dip can be whipped up in 5 minutes. I love it with raw carrots, celery, bell peppers, and cucumbers.

Prep time: 5 minutes *Cook time:* 0 minutes SERVES 4

- 1 (15-ounce) can no-salt-added cannellini beans, drained and rinsed
- 2 tablespoons olive oil
- 1 tablespoon low-fat plain Greek yogurt
- ¼ teaspoon salt
- ⅛ teaspoon paprika

Place the beans, olive oil, yogurt, and salt in a blender or food processor. Puree until smooth, about 1 minute. Transfer the puree to a serving dish and sprinkle with the paprika. Serve immediately, or cover and store in the refrigerator for up to 3 days.

SERVING SIZE: ¼ cup

NUTRITION INFORMATION (PER SERVING): Calories: 145; Total Fat: 8 grams; Saturated Fat: 1 gram; Protein: 5 grams; Total Carbohydrates: 14 grams; Sugars: 1 gram; Fiber: 4 grams; Cholesterol: 0 milligrams; Sodium: 181 milligrams

Baked Artichoke Dip with Fontina Cheese

A hot, cheesy artichoke dip always hits the spot, but who wants all those artery-clogging calories? This lightened-up dip is one of my favorites!

Prep time: 15 minutes *Cook time:* 30 minutes SERVES 10

- 1 clove garlic
- 2 (13.75-ounce) cans artichoke hearts
- 2 scallions
- ¼ cup nonfat plain Greek yogurt
- ¼ cup light mayonnaise
- 1½ ounces Fontina cheese, shredded (6 tablespoons)
- 1 teaspoon fresh lemon juice

Preheat the oven to 425°F.

Mince the garlic. Rinse, drain, and coarsely chop the artichoke hearts. Finely the chop scallions, both white and green parts.

In a medium bowl, combine the yogurt, mayonnaise, 3 tablespoon of the shredded cheese, the lemon juice, and the garlic. Add the artichokes and scallions, and stir to combine.

Place the yogurt mixture in an ovenproof bowl or ramekin, and sprinkle the remaining 3 tablespoons shredded cheese evenly over the top. Bake until the cheese is golden and bubbling, 30 minutes.

Remove from the oven and serve warm.

SERVING SIZE: ¼ cup

NUTRITION INFORMATION (PER SERVING): Calories: 62; Total Fat: 3 grams; Saturated Fat: 1 gram; Protein: 3 grams; Total Carbohydrates: 5 grams; Sugars: 1 gram; Fiber: 3 grams; Cholesterol: 7 milligrams; Sodium: 259 milligrams

Parsley Hummus

I grew up on hummus. I eat it at breakfast with my eggs, at lunch in my sandwich, and at dinner as an appetizer. This version is seasoned with flavorful parsley and can be used as a dip or a spread.

Prep time: 10 minutes *Cook time:* 0 minutes SERVES 6

- 1 (15-ounce can) chickpeas
- 1 clove garlic
- ¼ cup nonfat plain Greek yogurt
- ¼ cup coarsely chopped fresh parsley
- 3 tablespoons tahini
- 3 tablespoons fresh lemon juice
- ½ teaspoon salt
- ¼ teaspoon freshly ground black pepper
- 3 tablespoons extra-virgin olive oil

Drain and rinse the chickpeas. Mince the garlic.

Place the chickpeas and the yogurt in a food processor or blender and blend to combine. Add the garlic, parsley, tahini, lemon juice, salt, and pepper, and blend until smooth, about 30 seconds. With the machine running, gradually add the olive oil and blend until well incorporated.

Transfer the hummus to a serving bowl. Serve immediately, or cover and store in the refrigerator for up to 5 days.

Studies have found that rinsing canned beans cuts the sodium by up to 40%.

Tahini, also known as sesame seed paste, is a popular ingredient in Middle Eastern cuisine. I like Joyva or Roland.

SERVING SIZE: ¼ cup

NUTRITION INFORMATION (PER SERVING): Calories: 182; Total Fat: 12 grams; Saturated Fat: 2 grams; Protein: 6 grams; Total Carbohydrates: 15 grams; Sugars: 1 gram; Fiber: 4 grams; Cholesterol: 0 milligrams; Sodium: 218 milligrams

Babaganoush

This pureed eggplant dip is another traditional dish I grew up on. In my home, it is served as an appetizer with bread or with raw vegetables like carrots and celery. I have also discovered that babaganoush makes a darn tasty condiment for my turkey sandwiches. The possibilities are truly endless!

Prep time: 25 minutes, plus 2 hours refrigeration *Cook time:* 40 minutes SERVES 6

- Cooking spray
- 1 medium eggplant
- 2 cloves garlic
- ¼ cup fresh lemon juice (from about 2 lemons)
- 3 tablespoons tahini
- 3 tablespoons nonfat plain Greek yogurt
- ¼ teaspoon salt
- ¼ teaspoon freshly ground black pepper
- 1½ tablespoons olive oil

Preheat the oven to 400°F. Coat a baking sheet with cooking spray.

Halve the eggplant lengthwise and place the halves, cut side up, on the prepared baking sheet. Roast, turning occasionally, until soft, about 40 minutes. Remove from the oven and allow to cool for 15 minutes. Then scoop out the flesh with a spoon and discard the skin.

Mince the garlic. Place the roasted eggplant, garlic, lemon juice, tahini, yogurt, salt, and pepper in a food processor or blender and puree until smooth. With the machine running, slowly add the olive oil and blend until well incorporated.

Transfer the babaganoush to a serving bowl. Cover and refrigerate for at least 2 hours before serving, or for up to 5 days.

SERVING SIZE: ¼ cup

NUTRITION INFORMATION (PER SERVING): Calories: 99; Total Fat: 7 grams; Saturated Fat: 1 gram; Protein: 3 grams; Total Carbohydrates: 8 grams; Sugars: 2 grams; Fiber: 3 grams; Cholesterol: 0 milligrams; Sodium: 108 milligrams

Tzatziki with Pita Chips

Traditional cucumber-yogurt dip uses full-fat Greek yogurt to get its delicious texture, whereas some modern-day versions use boatloads of sour cream to create a rich flavor. In this recipe, a touch of reduced-fat sour cream is combined with nonfat Greek yogurt so you get a nice mix of both worlds.

Prep time: 15 minutes, plus 1 hour refrigeration *Cook time:* 10 minutes SERVES 6

FOR TZATZIKI

1 English cucumber

¾ cup nonfat plain Greek yogurt

1 clove garlic, minced

2 tablespoons chopped fresh dill

¼ cup reduced-fat sour cream

1 teaspoon fresh lemon juice

¼ teaspoon kosher salt

⅛ teaspoon freshly ground black pepper

FOR PITA CHIPS

3 (6½-inch) whole wheat pitas

2 tablespoons olive oil

¼ teaspoon kosher salt

To prepare the tzatziki: Peel and finely dice the cucumber. Using clean hands, squeeze out the excess liquid from the cucumber.

In a medium bowl, combine the cucumber with the yogurt. Stir in the garlic, dill, sour cream, lemon juice, salt, and pepper. Cover and refrigerate for 1 hour to marinate.

To make the pita chips: Preheat the oven to 400°F.

Cut each pita into 8 wedges and place them in an even layer on a baking sheet. In a small bowl, combine the olive oil and the salt. Brush this olive oil over both sides of the pita wedges. Toast in the oven until just browned, 10 minutes.

Let the pita chips cool slightly, and serve with the tzatziki.

SERVING SIZE: ¼ cup tzatziki and 4 pita chips

NUTRITION INFORMATION (PER SERVING): Calories: 150; Total Fat: 6 grams; Saturated Fat: 1 gram; Protein: 7 grams; Total Carbohydrates: 19 grams; Sugars: 3 grams; Fiber: 3 grams; Cholesterol: 5 milligrams; Sodium: 357 milligrams

Mango Guacamole

Step up your guacamole with a flavorful fruit! Made with mango, red onion, and red bell pepper, this guacamole creates a fiesta in your mouth that will leave you craving more.

Prep time: 20 minutes *Cook time:* 0 minutes SERVES 8

- 2 Hass avocados
- Juice of 1 lime
- 1 serrano chile
- 1 clove garlic
- ½ medium red onion
- ½ medium red bell pepper, seeded
- ¼ cup chopped fresh cilantro
- ½ cup nonfat plain Greek yogurt
- ½ teaspoon kosher salt
- ¼ teaspoon freshly ground black pepper
- 1 mango, peeled and cut into ¼-inch dice

Slice the avocados in half lengthwise and remove the pits. Scoop out the flesh and place it in a medium bowl. Add the lime juice.

Halve the serrano chile lengthwise. Discard the seeds and cut the chile into ⅛-inch dice. Mince the garlic. Peel and finely dice the red onion. Slice the red bell pepper in half, discard the seeds, and cut into ¼-inch dice. Add the chile, garlic, red onion, red bell pepper, cilantro, yogurt, salt, and black pepper to the avocado in the bowl, and stir to combine. Using a sharp knife, cut the avocado into a small dice. Gently stir in the mango, and serve.

SERVING SIZE: ½ cup

NUTRITION INFORMATION (PER SERVING): Calories: 116; Total Fat: 8 grams; Saturated Fat: 1 gram; Protein: 3 grams; Total Carbohydrates: 12 grams; Sugars: 6 grams; Fiber: 4 grams; Cholesterol: 0 milligrams; Sodium: 154 milligrams

Check avocados for ripeness by gently squeezing them. Don't apply pressure with your fingertips, as this can cause bruising. To speed up ripening, place hard avocados in a brown paper bag, add an apple or a banana, seal the bag, and set aside for 2 to 3 days.

Wasabi Sesame Dip

Jazz up Greek yogurt with flavorful Asian ingredients like wasabi and soy sauce. This dip is perfect to showcase with crudités made with cut-up raw carrots, cucumbers, and snow peas. I also like to serve it as a dipping sauce for dumplings, chicken satay, or Asian-style meatballs.

Prep time: 5 minutes *Cook time:* 5 minutes SERVES 8

- 2 tablespoons sesame seeds
- 2 cups nonfat plain Greek yogurt
- 8 teaspoons toasted sesame oil
- 4 teaspoons wasabi paste
- 4 teaspoons low-sodium soy sauce

Place the sesame seeds in a small pan and toast over medium heat until browned and fragrant, about 5 minutes. Remove from the heat and set aside.

In a small bowl, combine the yogurt, sesame oil, wasabi paste, and soy sauce. Place the dip in a serving bowl, and sprinkle the toasted sesame seeds over the top. Serve immediately or store in an airtight container in the refrigerator for up to 5 days.

SERVING SIZE: ¼ cup

NUTRITION INFORMATION (PER SERVING): Calories: 92; Total Fat: 6 grams; Saturated Fat: 1 gram; Protein: 7 grams; Total Carbohydrates: 4 grams; Sugars: 2 grams; Fiber: 0 grams; Cholesterol: 0 milligrams; Sodium: 111 milligrams

7-Layer Party Dip

This Mexican-inspired dip was devoured by my family when I recently served it for my brother's birthday. No one could believe it was *that* tasty for fewer than 250 calories per serving! With its seven layers of deliciousness, you'll be drooling while preparing it.

Prep time: 20 minutes *Cook time:* 45 minutes SERVES 8

- ½ cup long-grain brown rice
- 2 tablespoons chopped fresh cilantro
- 1 medium onion
- 1 (15-ounce) can low-sodium black beans
- 1 tablespoon olive oil
- 1 teaspoon hot sauce
- ½ teaspoon ground cumin
- 2 tablespoons chopped fresh chives
- 1 cup nonfat plain Greek yogurt
- ½ teaspoon grated lime zest
- 1 avocado
- 1 jalapeño pepper
- 1 tablespoon fresh lime juice
- ½ teaspoon kosher salt
- 3 tomatillos
- ¼ teaspoon freshly ground black pepper
- 3 ounces (¾ cup) pitted black olives
- 4 ounces (1 cup) shredded light Mexican cheese blend

In a medium pot over high heat, bring 1 cup water to a boil. Add the rice and return to a boil; then lower the heat and cover the pot. Simmer, covered, until the rice is tender and the water has been absorbed, about 40 minutes. Fluff the rice with a fork and stir in the cilantro. Place the rice in an even layer on the bottom of a deep casserole or baking dish.

Peel and chop the onion. Drain and rinse the black beans. In a medium skillet, heat the olive oil over medium heat. Add the onion and cook until translucent, about 2 minutes. Mix in the black beans and cook until warmed through, about 1 minute. Stir in the hot sauce and cumin. Layer the bean mixture on top of the rice.

In a small bowl, combine the chives, yogurt, and lime zest. Set aside.

Slice the avocado in half lengthwise and remove the pit. Scoop out the flesh and place it in a small bowl. Halve the jalapeño lengthwise, discard the seeds, and cut into ⅛-inch dice. Add the jalapeño, lime juice, and ¼ teaspoon of the salt to the avocado in the bowl. Mash with a fork until well combined. Set aside.

Chop the tomatillos. Place them in a small bowl and toss with the remaining ¼ teaspoon salt and the black pepper.

Thinly slice the olives. Spread the yogurt mixture over the beans in an even layer. Then spread the avocado mixture evenly over the yogurt. Sprinkle with the cheese, then the tomatillo mixture. Finally, top with the sliced black olives.

Serve immediately, or cover and store in the refrigerator for up to 3 days.

SERVING SIZE: 1 cup

NUTRITION INFORMATION (PER SERVING): Calories: 237; Total Fat: 11 grams; Saturated Fat: 2 grams; Protein: 12 grams; Total Carbohydrates: 25 grams; Sugars: 4 grams; Fiber: 6 grams; Cholesterol: 10 milligrams; Sodium: 340 milligrams

Asian Lettuce Cups with Broccoli Slaw and Chicken

Always one of my favorites to order at a restaurant, Asian lettuce cups are typically brimming with sodium and oozing with fat. Making your own is just as tasty, but you have full control over the ingredients.

Prep time: 30 minutes, plus 1 hour refrigeration *Cook time:* 10 minutes SERVES 8

- 8 ounces boneless, skinless chicken breast
- ½ jalapeño pepper, cut into ⅛-inch dice
- 1½ tablespoons packed dark brown sugar
- 1 tablespoon low-sodium soy sauce
- 1 tablespoon fresh lemon juice
- 1 teaspoon Dijon mustard
- ⅓ cup natural creamy peanut butter
- 2 tablespoons fresh lime juice
- 1 teaspoon fish sauce
- 1 teaspoon Sriracha sauce
- 1 clove garlic, grated
- ½ teaspoon grated fresh ginger
- ⅓ cup nonfat plain Greek yogurt
- ¼ cup chopped fresh mint leaves
- ¼ cup chopped fresh basil leaves
- 1 (10-ounce) bag broccoli slaw (4 cups)
- Cooking spray
- 2 heads Bibb lettuce

Place the chicken between layers of plastic wrap. Using a mallet, pound the chicken to an even ½-inch thickness. In a large bowl, combine the jalapeño, brown sugar, soy sauce, lemon juice, and mustard to make the marinade. Place the chicken in the marinade, being sure to coat it completely. Cover and refrigerate for at least 1 hour or as long as 8 hours.

Meanwhile, in a large bowl, combine ½ cup water with the peanut butter, lime juice, fish sauce, Sriracha, garlic, and ginger. Whisk together until smooth. Add the yogurt and continue to stir until well combined. Add the mint, basil, and broccoli slaw to the bowl and toss to combine.

Coat a grill pan with cooking spray and heat it over medium-high heat. When the oil is shimmering, add the chicken, discarding the excess marinade, and cook, turning the pieces over halfway through,

If you don't have a mallet to pound your chicken (or any other meat), don't worry! You can use a rolling pin, the edge of a heavy pan, or a 16-ounce can.

until browned, 10 minutes. Remove from the pan and set aside to cool for 10 minutes. Then cut or tear the chicken into at least 16 bite-size pieces.

To assemble, create cups with leaves of the Bibb lettuce. Place 2 tablespoons of the slaw into each cup and top with 1 piece of chicken.

SERVING SIZE: 2 lettuce cups

NUTRITION INFORMATION (PER SERVING): Calories: 126; Total Fat: 6 grams; Saturated Fat: 1 gram; Protein: 11 grams; Total Carbohydrates: 8 grams; Sugars: 5 grams; Fiber: 2 grams; Cholesterol: 18 milligrams; Sodium: 213 milligrams

Spiced Almond, Cheese, and Rosemary Phyllo Cups

Spiced nuts just got a makeover. The combination of rosemary and cayenne gives these nuts a spicy zing, while the creamy cheese soothes the punch. Packaged in neat little phyllo cups, these will be a conversation piece at any gathering.

Prep time: 25 minutes *Cook time:* 10 minutes SERVES 8

- ¾ cup raw or blanched almonds
- 1 tablespoon olive oil
- 1 tablespoon chopped fresh rosemary
- ½ teaspoon salt
- ¼ teaspoon cayenne pepper
- ⅛ teaspoon freshly ground black pepper
- 2 cloves garlic
- 8 ounces Neufchâtel cheese, at room temperature
- ¾ cup nonfat plain Greek yogurt
- 1 tablespoon grated lemon zest
- 2 tablespoons fresh lemon juice
- 24 precooked phyllo cups (I like Athens)

Preheat the oven to 375°F.

In a small bowl, combine the almonds, olive oil, chopped rosemary, ¼ teaspoon of the salt, cayenne, and black pepper. Toss to combine. Spread the almonds in an even layer on a baking sheet. Toast until lightly browned and fragrant, about 10 minutes. Set aside to cool for 5 minutes; then coarsely chop. Grate the garlic cloves into a medium bowl. Add the Neufchâtel cheese, yogurt, lemon zest, lemon juice, and the remaining ¼ teaspoon of the salt, and stir to combine.

To assemble, place 1 heaping teaspoon of the cheese mixture in each phyllo cup, and sprinkle with 1½ teaspoons of the chopped almonds.

SERVING SIZE: 3 phyllo cups

NUTRITION INFORMATION (PER SERVING): Calories: 224; Total Fat: 17 grams; Saturated Fat: 4 grams; Protein: 10 grams; Total Carbohydrates: 13 grams; Sugars: 2 grams; Fiber: 2 grams; Cholesterol: 21 milligrams; Sodium: 279 milligrams

The cheese filling can be made a day in advance and kept, covered, in the refrigerator until ready to use. The nuts can also be prepared in advance and kept in an airtight container for up to 4 days.

These yummy spiced nuts can be enjoyed as a snack on their own.

Salmon and Dill Cucumber Bites

I always look forward to attending cocktail parties, but the high-calorie appetizers are a buzzkill. Why can't finger foods be delicious *and* low in calories? Now they can!

Prep time: 20 minutes *Cook time:* 0 minutes SERVES 6

- ¾ English cucumber
- 1¼ ounces smoked salmon
- ¼ cup low-fat plain Greek yogurt
- ¼ cup whipped cream cheese
- 1 tablespoon chopped fresh dill

Slice the cucumber into twenty-four ¼-inch-thick rounds. Arrange the cucumber slices on a large serving platter. Cut the salmon into 24 bite-size pieces.

In a small bowl, fold the yogurt and cream cheese together until thoroughly combined. Then add the dill and stir to incorporate.

Top each cucumber slice with 1 teaspoon of the yogurt-cheese mixture, then 1 piece of the salmon. Serve immediately.

SERVING SIZE: 4 pieces

NUTRITION INFORMATION (PER SERVING): Calories: 38; Total Fat: 3 grams; Saturated Fat: 1 gram; Protein: 2 grams; Total Carbohydrates: 3 grams; Sugars: 1 gram; Fiber: 0 grams; Cholesterol: 9 milligrams; Sodium: 80 milligrams

Farro and Pea Shooters with Lime Dressing

Served in shot glasses, the brown, green, and purples hues in this dish appeal to the eyes, while the zesty lime dressing appeals to the palate. It's easy to make and even more fun to eat.

Prep time: 15 minutes *Cook time:* 30 minutes SERVES 8

- ½ cup farro
- ½ cup frozen green peas
- 4 medium radishes, cut into ⅛-inch dice
- ½ jalapeño pepper, cut into ⅛-inch dice
- ¼ cup fresh lime juice (from 2 limes)
- ½ teaspoon hot sauce
- ¼ teaspoon salt
- ¼ teaspoon freshly ground black pepper
- 2 tablespoons nonfat plain Greek yogurt
- 6 tablespoons chopped fresh cilantro

Combine 1½ cups water and the farro in a medium pot and bring to a boil over high heat. Turn the heat to low, cover the pot, and simmer until the water has been absorbed and the farro is al dente, about 30 minutes. Then remove the pot from the heat and set it aside to cool for 10 minutes.

Meanwhile, cook the peas according to the package directions, on the stove or in the microwave.

In a medium bowl, combine the farro, peas, diced radishes, and diced jalapeño. Set aside.

In a small bowl, whisk together the lime juice, hot sauce, salt, and black pepper. Add the yogurt and continue to whisk until smooth.

Spoon 2 tablespoons of the farro mixture into each of sixteen shot glasses. Top each one with 1 teaspoon of the lime dressing and then about 1 teaspoon of the chopped cilantro.

SERVING SIZE: 2 shooters

NUTRITION INFORMATION (PER SERVING): Calories: 54; Total Fat: 0 grams; Saturated Fat: 0 grams; Protein: 3 grams; Total Carbohydrates: 11 grams; Sugars: 1 gram; Fiber: 2 grams; Cholesterol: 0 milligrams; Sodium: 102 milligrams

Farro is an ancient grain that is an excellent source of fiber and a good source of iron. Cook it as you would rice, with a ratio of 1 cup dry farro to 3 cups water.

Herbed Goat Cheese and Red Pepper Crostini

This delicious snack has a flavorful kick and a gorgeous hue. It's sure to please!

Prep time: 15 minutes *Cook time:* 10 minutes SERVES 8

- ½ whole-grain baguette (8 ounces)
- 5 tablespoons olive oil
- ½ teaspoon kosher salt
- 5½ ounces jarred fire-roasted red bell peppers (about 1½ peppers)
- 2 scallions
- 4 ounces soft goat cheese (I like Chavrie)
- 2 tablespoons nonfat plain Greek yogurt
- 2 teaspoons fresh thyme leaves
- ⅛ teaspoon freshly ground black pepper

Preheat the oven to 400°F.

Cut the baguette into twenty-four ¼-inch-thick slices. Arrange them in an even layer on a baking sheet.

In a small bowl, combine the olive oil and salt. Brush the oil over both sides of the baguette slices. Bake, turning the slices over halfway through, until the bread is golden brown, about 10 minutes.

Meanwhile, slice the red peppers lengthwise into twenty-four ¾-inch-wide slivers. Chop the scallions, both white and green parts. In a medium bowl, combine the chopped scallions, goat cheese, yogurt, thyme, and black pepper.

To assemble, spread about 1 teaspoon of the cheese mixture over a piece of toasted baguette. Fold a red pepper over the cheese. Repeat with the remaining ingredients, and serve.

SERVING SIZE: 3 crostini

NUTRITION INFORMATION (PER SERVING): Calories: 193; Total Fat: 12 grams; Saturated Fat: 3 grams; Protein: 6 grams; Total Carbohydrates: 16 grams; Sugars: 2 grams; Fiber: 2 grams; Cholesterol: 7 milligrams; Sodium: 403 milligrams

Green Goddess Deviled Eggs

Fill deviled eggs with green goddess flavors for one heck of an appetizer. This recipe maintains that beloved creamy texture without overloading on artery-clogging fat.

Prep time: 15 minutes *Cook time:* 20 minutes SERVES 6

- 6 large eggs
- 1 scallion
- 1 clove garlic
- ½ Hass avocado
- 2 tablespoons chopped fresh parsley, plus extra leaves for garnish
- 2 tablespoons chopped fresh basil
- 2 tablespoons nonfat plain Greek yogurt
- 1 tablespoon light mayonnaise
- 2 teaspoons fresh lemon juice
- ¼ teaspoon salt
- ⅛ teaspoon freshly ground black pepper

Place the eggs in a large pot and cover with cold water. Place the pot over high heat, bring to a boil, and cook for 3 minutes. Then remove from the heat, cover, and allow to stand for 15 minutes. Drain, and run cold water over the eggs until they are completely cool, about 10 minutes. Once they have cooled, peel the eggs and cut them in half lengthwise. Remove the yolks and set 3 aside; discard the remainder of the yolks or save them for another use.

Chop the scallion, both white and green parts. Mince the garlic. In a food processor, combine the 3 egg yolks, the chopped scallion, garlic, avocado, parsley, basil, yogurt, mayonnaise, lemon juice, salt, and pepper. Puree until smooth.

Place the mixture in a pastry bag or a plastic sandwich bag with one corner snipped off, and pipe about 1 tablespoon into each egg half. Garnish each one with a parsley leaf. Serve within 1 hour of preparation.

SERVING SIZE: 2 halves

NUTRITION INFORMATION (PER SERVING): Calories: 88; Total Fat: 6 grams; Saturated Fat: 1 gram; Protein: 6 grams; Total Carbohydrates: 3 grams; Sugars: 1 gram; Fiber: 2 grams; Cholesterol: 94 milligrams; Sodium: 182 milligrams

Roasted Shrimp Cocktail with Thousand Island Dressing

Shrimp is a very lean protein, with 3 ounces providing 80 calories, 1 gram of fat, and 18 grams of protein. It's also an excellent source of selenium and a good source of vitamins D and B_{12}. When cocktail sauce sounds boring, complement this good-for-you finger food with a mouthwatering low-calorie version of Thousand Island dressing.

Prep time: 15 minutes *Cook time:* 5 minutes SERVES 8

FOR SHRIMP

1 pound (8 to 10) jumbo shrimp
½ teaspoon salt
¼ teaspoon freshly ground black pepper
4 teaspoons olive oil
4 teaspoons fresh lemon juice

FOR THOUSAND ISLAND DRESSING

2 cloves garlic
½ cup low-fat plain Greek yogurt
½ cup light mayonnaise
¼ cup low-fat milk
2 tablespoons ketchup
2 teaspoons Worcestershire sauce
1 teaspoon Sriracha sauce
¼ teaspoon salt
4 teaspoons sweet pickle relish

To cook the shrimp: Preheat the oven to 400°F. Season the shrimp all over with the salt and pepper. In a small bowl, toss the shrimp with the olive oil and lemon juice. Arrange the shrimp in an even layer on a baking sheet and roast until pink and cooked through, 5 to 6 minutes.

To make the Thousand Island dressing: Mince the garlic. Place the garlic, yogurt, mayonnaise, milk, ketchup, Worcestershire sauce, Sriracha, and salt into a small bowl. Stir together until smooth and evenly combined. Add the sweet pickle relish and stir to incorporate.

Serve the shrimp warm with Thousand Island dressing on the side.

SERVING SIZE: 2 to 3 shrimp and 2 tablespoons dressing

NUTRITION INFORMATION (PER SERVING): Calories: 134; Total Fat: 8 grams; Saturated Fat: 1 gram; Protein: 10 grams; Total Carbohydrates: 5 grams; Sugars: 4 grams; Fiber: 0 grams; Cholesterol: 78 milligrams; Sodium: 619 milligrams

Studies have found that saturated fat, not cholesterol, has the greater impact on raising "bad" LDL cholesterol. Shrimp contains minimal saturated fat, so enjoy it in moderation.

Mascarpone-Stuffed Mushrooms

The flavor of these mushrooms complements the combination of mascarpone and Parmesan cheeses, making it a perfect starter for fewer than 100 calories apiece.

Prep time: 15 minutes *Cook time:* 15 minutes SERVES 8

- Cooking spray
- ½ cup whole wheat panko breadcrumbs
- ½ cup mascarpone cheese
- ¼ cup nonfat plain Greek yogurt
- 1 large egg, beaten
- 2 tablespoons grated Parmesan cheese
- ½ teaspoon dried parsley
- ⅛ teaspoon salt
- ⅛ teaspoon freshly ground black pepper
- 8 large white mushrooms

Preheat the oven to 375°F. Coat a baking sheet with cooking spray and set it aside.

In a medium bowl, stir together the panko breadcrumbs, mascarpone cheese, yogurt, egg, Parmesan cheese, parsley, salt, and pepper.

Wash the mushrooms and remove the stems. Arrange the mushrooms, gill side up, in an even layer on the prepared baking sheet. Stuff each mushroom with 2 tablespoons of the cheese mixture. Bake until the mushrooms are fragrant and lightly browned, about 15 minutes. Remove the baking sheet from the oven and set aside to cool for 5 minutes. Serve warm.

SERVING SIZE: 1 stuffed mushroom

NUTRITION INFORMATION (PER SERVING): Calories: 90; Total Fat: 6 grams; Saturated Fat: 4 grams; Protein: 4 grams; Total Carbohydrates: 5 grams; Sugars: 1 gram; Fiber: 1 gram; Cholesterol: 38 milligrams; Sodium: 88 milligrams

To wash mushrooms, lightly rinse them with cold water and immediately pat dry with a paper towel; or use a damp paper towel to wipe them, one at a time, to remove any dirt. Whatever you do, don't soak them! Mushrooms absorb water like a sponge and won't brown well if they're soggy.

Sesame-Ginger Salmon Croquettes with Sriracha Cream

These tasty bites combine a ton of flavors to complement the salmon. They are a definite crowd-pleaser at any gathering.

Prep time: 20 minutes, plus 20 minutes refrigeration *Cook time:* 16 minutes SERVES 6

FOR CROQUETTES

1 scallion
2 tablespoons toasted sesame oil
2 tablespoons nonfat plain Greek yogurt
1 large egg
1 large egg white
2 teaspoons Dijon mustard
1 teaspoon grated fresh ginger
¼ teaspoon salt
¼ teaspoon freshly ground black pepper
1 pound fresh salmon
¾ cup whole wheat panko breadcrumbs

FOR SRIRACHA CREAM

¾ cup nonfat plain Greek yogurt
¼ cup light mayonnaise
1 tablespoon Sriracha sauce

2 tablespoons canola oil

Prepare the croquettes: Chop the scallion, both white and green parts. In a medium bowl, whisk together the sesame oil, yogurt, chopped scallion, egg, egg white, mustard, ginger, salt, and pepper. Using a sharp knife, remove the skin from the salmon; then dice the flesh into 1-inch cubes. Add the salmon to the yogurt mixture, along with the panko breadcrumbs. Toss gently to coat and combine. Transfer the fish mixture to a blender or food processor, and pulse 10 to 12 times, just until the fish is finely minced and the mixture is well combined.

Scoop out 1 tablespoon of the fish mixture, and using clean hands, form it into a patty. Place it on a large plate or a platter, gently pressing down with the palm of your hand to flatten it slightly. Repeat to make 12 small patties. Cover the platter with plastic wrap and refrigerate for at least 20 minutes or up to 1 hour.

Meanwhile, make the Sriracha cream: Stir the yogurt, mayonnaise, and Sriracha together in a small bowl. Cover with plastic wrap and refrigerate for at least 10 minutes or up to 1 hour.

Research has shown that consuming two servings of salmon each week may help lower your risk of having a heart attack by 27%.

Cook the croquettes: In a large pan, heat the canola oil over medium heat. When the oil is shimmering, add 6 croquettes, leaving about 1 inch all around each. Sauté until golden brown, about 4 minutes per side. Transfer the croquettes to a plate or platter. Cover with aluminum foil to keep warm, and repeat with the remaining patties.

Spoon 1 tablespoon Sriracha cream over each finished croquette, and serve warm.

SERVING SIZE: 2 croquettes and 2 tablespoons Sriracha cream

NUTRITION INFORMATION (PER SERVING): Calories: 333; Total Fat: 24 grams; Saturated Fat: 4 grams; Protein: 21 grams; Total Carbohydrates: 9 grams; Sugars: 2 grams; Fiber: 0 grams; Cholesterol: 76 milligrams; Sodium: 346 milligrams

Maple-Cayenne Baked Meatballs with Sun-Dried Tomato Dip

Serve these babies at your next gathering and you may have to disclose two secrets: First, the sweet flavor comes from maple syrup (only 2 tablespoons for the whole batch!). Second, half the beef was replaced with sautéed mushrooms and shallots, making these meatballs both healthy and delicious.

Prep time: 15 minutes *Cook time:* 30 minutes SERVES 8

FOR MEATBALLS

Cooking spray
1 shallot
1 portobello mushroom cap
2 teaspoons olive oil
½ cup fresh parsley
8 ounces 90% lean ground beef
½ cup whole wheat panko breadcrumbs
2 tablespoons pure maple syrup
¼ cup plain nonfat Greek yogurt
1 tablespoon Marsala wine
1 large egg, beaten
⅛ teaspoon cayenne pepper
½ teaspoon salt
⅛ teaspoon freshly ground black pepper

FOR SUN-DRIED TOMATO DIP

6 sun-dried tomatoes packed in olive oil
1 cup nonfat plain Greek yogurt
¼ teaspoon salt
¼ teaspoon freshly ground black pepper

Make the meatballs: Preheat the oven to 400°F. Coat a 24-cup mini muffin tin with cooking spray and set it aside.

Chop the shallot. Finely dice the portobello mushroom cap. In a medium saucepan, heat the olive oil over medium heat. When the oil is shimmering, add the chopped shallots and sauté until soft and translucent, 2 minutes. Add the diced mushrooms and cook until they are browned and their liquid is released and evaporated, about 5 minutes. Set aside to cool for 5 minutes.

Chop the parsley. In a large bowl, using clean hands, combine the parsley, sautéed shallot and mushrooms, ground beef, panko breadcrumbs, maple syrup, yogurt, wine, egg, cayenne, salt, and pepper. Scoop out a heaping spoonful of the mixture, shape it into a round ball, and place it in a prepared muffin cup. Repeat to make 24 meatballs. Bake until browned on the outside and cooked through, 20 minutes. Remove the muffin tin from the oven and allow to cool for about 5 minutes.

Meanwhile, prepare the dip: Place the tomatoes, yogurt, salt, and pepper in a blender or food processor, and blend until smooth.

Place the meatballs on a plate or serving platter, and serve warm with the dip on the side.

SERVING SIZE: 3 meatballs and 2 tablespoons dip

NUTRITION INFORMATION (PER SERVING): Calories: 112; Total Fat: 4 grams; Saturated Fat: 1 gram; Protein: 10 grams; Carbohydrates: 10 grams; Sugars: 4 grams; Fiber: 0 grams; Cholesterol: 45 milligrams; Sodium: 188 milligrams

Spanakopita

You *can* eat your Greek spinach pie and have a slim figure too! Although this traditional dish can clock in at close to 600 calories per slice, using Greek yogurt can bring it down to just around 200 per serving.

Prep time: 30 minutes *Cook time:* 40 minutes SERVES 12

- Cooking spray
- 1 large yellow onion
- 8 scallions
- 3 pounds frozen chopped spinach, thawed and drained
- 4 tablespoons olive oil
- 2 cups chopped fresh dill
- 2 cups nonfat plain Greek yogurt
- 3 large eggs, beaten
- 8 ounces feta cheese, crumbled
- 10 sheets phyllo dough (thawed if frozen)

Preheat the oven to 400°F. Coat a 13 x 9-inch baking dish with cooking spray and set it aside.

Do not worry if the phyllo does not fit neatly or if the dough rips. The taste matters more than the appearance for this one!

The spanakopita squares hold together best if you slice it in the baking dish before *baking. Without pre-slicing, the spanakopita tends to fall apart easily and becomes messy when you try to serve it.*

Peel and chop the onion. Chop the scallions, both white and green parts. Squeeze the liquid from the spinach.

Heat 2 tablespoons of the olive oil in a large sauté pan over medium heat. When the oil is shimmering, add the chopped onion and scallions and cook until softened and translucent, 4 minutes. Add the spinach and cook until warmed through, 5 minutes. Remove the pan from the heat and set aside to cool for about 15 minutes. Then add the chopped dill and stir to combine.

In a medium bowl, whisk the yogurt and eggs together. Add the feta and stir to combine. Pour the yogurt mixture into the spinach mixture in the pan, and stir carefully to combine.

To assemble the pie, place 1 sheet of the phyllo dough on the bottom of the prepared baking dish, folding in the edges if necessary to fit. Using a pastry brush, carefully brush some of the remaining 2 tablespoons of olive oil over the dough. Place another sheet of dough on top, and repeat this process for a total of 5 sheets, brushing olive oil over each piece of phyllo dough.

Spoon the spinach filling over the phyllo dough and spread it out in an even layer. Place a layer of phyllo dough over the spinach, and repeat the procedure of oiling and stacking the dough for a total of 5 layers. Tuck any loose edges down into the sides of the dish. Finish the top layer by brushing it with the remaining olive oil.

Using a sharp paring knife, cut 4 even rows along the long dimension, then 3 along the short dimension, making a total of 12 squares. Be sure to cut down through to the bottom layer of dough.

Place the baking dish in the center of the oven and bake until the top is golden brown, approximately 40 minutes. Remove from the oven and allow to cool for 10 minutes before serving. Cover any leftover spanakopita with plastic wrap and store it in the refrigerator for up to 5 days.

SERVING SIZE: 1 (3 × 3-inch) piece

NUTRITION INFORMATION (PER SERVING): Calories: 211; Total Fat: 11 grams; Saturated Fat: 4 grams; Protein: 12 grams; Total Carbohydrates: 15 grams; Sugars: 4 grams; Fiber: 4 grams; Cholesterol: 63 milligrams; Sodium: 480 milligrams

CHAPTER 4

Salads, Soups, and Sandwiches

SALADS

SOUPS

SANDWICHES

Joe's Chopped Salad

My grandpa Joe made this salad for lunch and dinner every day. But instead of Greek yogurt, his version had about ¾ cup of regular mayonnaise and a ton of salt. To honor his memory (he lived until he was ninety-two!), I created this lightened version of his favorite meal.

Prep time: 15 minutes *Cook time:* 0 minutes SERVES 6

1 romaine lettuce heart
2 medium plum tomatoes
6 Kirby or Persian cucumbers
1 yellow bell pepper
3 tablespoons canola oil mayonnaise
3 tablespoons nonfat plain Greek yogurt
1½ teaspoons fresh lemon juice
¼ teaspoon kosher salt
¼ teaspoon freshly ground black pepper

Coarsely chop the romaine. Finely chop the tomatoes. Cut the cucumbers into ¼-inch dice. Cut the yellow bell pepper in half, discard the seeds, and cut into ¼-inch dice. Place the lettuce and vegetables in a large bowl and toss to combine.

In a small bowl, stir together the mayonnaise, yogurt, lemon juice, salt, and black pepper. Add the dressing to the salad and toss to coat evenly.

SERVING SIZE: 1 cup

NUTRITION INFORMATION (PER SERVING): Calories: 75; Total Fat: 6 grams; Saturated Fat: 1 gram; Protein: 2 grams; Total Carbohydrates: 5 grams; Sugars: 3 grams; Fiber: 1 gram; Cholesterol: 3 milligrams; Sodium: 152 milligrams

Salad Parfait

Want to impress your family and friends? Create these stunning salad parfaits. The layers of brightly colored vegetables and herbed Greek yogurt are breathtaking.

Prep time: 20 minutes *Cook time:* 0 minutes SERVES 4

- ½ cup nonfat plain Greek yogurt
- 2 tablespoons chopped fresh basil
- 2 tablespoons chopped fresh parsley
- 1 clove garlic
- 2 tablespoons white balsamic vinegar
- ¼ teaspoon mustard powder
- ¼ teaspoon kosher salt
- ¼ teaspoon freshly ground black pepper
- ¼ cup extra-virgin olive oil
- 2 plum tomatoes
- 2 Kirby or Persian cucumbers
- ¼ head romaine lettuce
- 1 yellow bell pepper
- 2 medium carrots

Put the yogurt in a medium bowl, add the basil and parsley, and stir to combine. Set aside.

Mince the garlic. In a medium bowl, whisk together the garlic, vinegar, mustard powder, salt, and black pepper. While whisking, slowly drizzle in the olive oil until emulsified.

Cut the tomatoes and cucumbers into ¼-inch dice; you should have about 1 cup of each. Shred the romaine. Cut the yellow bell pepper in half, discard the seeds, and cut into ¼-inch dice. Peel and grate the carrots.

To assemble the parfaits, layer the bottom of each of four parfait glasses with ¼ cup diced tomatoes, followed by ¼ cup diced cucumbers and ½ cup shredded lettuce. Gently press down with the back of a spoon to pack the ingredients. Top with 2 tablespoons of the yogurt mixture, ¼ cup of the diced yellow pepper, and then ¼ cup of the shredded carrots. Drizzle with 1½ tablespoons of the vinaigrette.

Salad dressings are generally made with oil and vinegar. But since oil and vinegar don't mix, we need to emulsify—that is, combine two foods that naturally don't mix. To do this, slowly add the oil to the vinegar while vigorously whisking or while blending in a food processor or blender.

SERVING SIZE: 1 parfait

NUTRITION INFORMATION (PER SERVING): Calories: 168; Total Fat: 14 grams; Saturated Fat: 2 grams; Protein: 4 grams; Total Carbohydrates: 9 grams; Sugars: 4 grams; Fiber: 2 grams; Cholesterol: 0 milligrams; Sodium: 166 milligrams

Arugula Salad with Pomegranate Dressing

The sweet and tangy pomegranate dressing complements a simple four-ingredient salad. Make a double batch of the dressing and use it to marinate chicken or pork!

Prep time: 10 minutes *Cook time:* 8 minutes SERVES 4

FOR SALAD

¼ cup (1 ounce) chopped raw walnuts
6 cups (7 ounces) arugula
½ small red onion, thinly sliced
½ cup pomegranate seeds

FOR DRESSING

2 tablespoons olive oil
2 tablespoons red wine vinegar
1 tablespoon unsulphured molasses
1 tablespoon pomegranate juice
¼ teaspoon salt
⅛ teaspoon ground cinnamon
¼ cup nonfat plain Greek yogurt

Preheat the oven to 350°F. Place the walnuts in an even layer on a baking sheet and toast until fragrant and lightly browned, about 8 minutes. Remove the baking sheet from the oven and set aside to cool.

Meanwhile, prepare the dressing: In a small bowl, whisk together the olive oil, vinegar, molasses, pomegranate juice, salt, and cinnamon. Whisk in the yogurt until well incorporated.

Place the arugula in a large salad bowl. Add the onion, pomegranate seeds, and toasted walnuts. Serve the salad with the dressing on the side.

SERVING SIZE: 1½ cups salad and 2½ tablespoons dressing

NUTRITION INFORMATION (PER SERVING): Calories: 173; Total Fat: 12 grams; Saturated Fat: 2 grams; Protein: 4 grams; Total Carbohydrates: 15 grams; Sugars: 9 grams; Fiber: 3 grams; Cholesterol: 0 milligrams; Sodium: 173 milligrams

Molasses is a wonderful addition to your repertoire of sweeteners. It contains vitamins and minerals like vitamin B_6, magnesium, iron, potassium, copper, and selenium. As with any sweetener, use it in small amounts.

Greek Salad with Feta Dressing

Many traditional Greek salads are made with mounds of feta and buckets of high-calorie dressing. In this recipe, just one ounce of the star cheese is used. It keeps fat and calories in check without compromising flavor.

Prep time: 25 minutes *Cook time:* 0 minutes SERVES 4

FOR SALAD

1½ cups grape tomatoes
2 cucumbers
½ cup pitted kalamata olives
¼ red onion
6 cups shredded romaine lettuce

FOR DRESSING

1 ounce feta cheese, crumbled (about 3 tablespoons)
2 tablespoons low-fat milk
1 tablespoon low-fat plain Greek yogurt
1 tablespoon olive oil
½ clove garlic
¼ teaspoon dried oregano
⅛ teaspoon salt

To make the salad: Slice the grape tomatoes in half lengthwise. Peel the cucumbers and cut into ½-inch dice. Halve the kalamata olives. Cut the red onion into ¼-inch dice. Place the vegetables and olives in a large salad bowl, add the lettuce, and toss. Set aside.

To make the dressing: Place the feta, milk, yogurt, olive oil, garlic, oregano, and salt in a blender or food processor. Blend until smooth, about 2 minutes.

Place about 2½ cups of the salad into each of four salad bowls. Top each with 1½ tablespoons of the dressing and toss to combine. Serve immediately.

SERVING SIZE: 2½ cups salad and 1½ tablespoons dressing

NUTRITION INFORMATION (PER SERVING): Calories: 114; Total Fat: 8 grams; Saturated Fat: 2 grams; Protein: 4 grams; Total Carbohydrates: 7 grams; Sugars: 4 grams; Fiber: 3 grams; Cholesterol: 7 milligrams; Sodium: 449 milligrams

Spinach Salad with Orange-Ginger Dressing

My father loves anything with a tangy orange flavor. I combined that with his other favorite ingredients in his honor.

Prep time: 15 minutes *Cook time:* 0 minutes SERVES 4

FOR SALAD

1 bunch (about ⅓ pound) fresh spinach
6 ounces cherry tomatoes
1 (6-ounce) can pitted black olives
4 Kirby or Persian cucumbers
2 medium carrots
⅓ cup unsalted shelled pumpkin seeds

FOR DRESSING

½ teaspoon grated orange zest
2 tablespoons fresh orange juice
1 teaspoon honey
¼ teaspoon salt
⅛ teaspoon ground ginger
⅛ teaspoon ground cinnamon
½ cup nonfat plain Greek yogurt

Remove the stems from the spinach and tear the leaves into bite-size pieces.

Slice the cherry tomatoes in half lengthwise. Slice the black olives in half lengthwise. Slice the cucumbers in half lengthwise, then into ¼-inch-thick half-moons. Peel and grate the carrots. Place all the vegetables, the olives, and the pumpkin seeds in a large bowl and toss to combine.

To make the dressing: Whisk the orange zest, orange juice, honey, salt, ginger, and cinnamon together in a small bowl. Whisk in the yogurt until well combined.

Place 2 cups of the salad in each of four salad bowls. Top each serving with 2 tablespoons of the dressing, and toss to combine. Serve immediately.

SERVING SIZE: 2 cups salad and 2 tablespoons dressing

NUTRITION INFORMATION (PER SERVING): Calories: 194; Total Fat: 13 grams; Saturated Fat: 1 gram; Protein: 9 grams; Total Carbohydrates: 16 grams; Sugars: 7 grams; Fiber: 3 grams; Cholesterol: 0 milligrams; Sodium: 548 milligrams

Cobb Salad with Creamy Dill Dressing

The Cobb was always one of my go-to salads when dining out, but I stopped ordering it after restaurants started posting their nutrition information—I realized I was eating salads containing 700 to 1,000 calories or even more! I now opt to make my own version so I have full control over the contents and the portions. The total calories in this Cobb are a mere fraction of what I was eating out!

Prep time: 25 minutes *Cook time:* 15 minutes SERVES 4

FOR SALAD

2 large eggs
8 ounces boneless, skinless chicken breasts
⅛ teaspoon salt
⅛ teaspoon freshly ground black pepper
1 clove garlic
1 teaspoon olive oil
1 teaspoon fresh lemon juice
1 head green-leaf lettuce
4 ounces Black Forest ham
2 medium plum tomatoes
1 avocado

FOR DRESSING

2 scallions
1 clove garlic
2 tablespoons chopped fresh dill
¾ cup low-fat buttermilk
3 tablespoons nonfat plain Greek yogurt
3 tablespoons light mayonnaise
½ teaspoon fresh lemon juice
⅛ teaspoon salt
⅛ teaspoon freshly ground black pepper

To start the salad: Place the eggs in a large pot and cover with cold water. Place the pot over high heat and bring to a boil; cook for 3 minutes. Then remove from the heat, cover the pot, and allow to stand for 15 minutes. Drain, and run cold water over the eggs until completely cool, about 10 minutes. Once they have cooled, peel and slice the eggs. Set them aside.

Place the chicken breasts between two pieces of plastic wrap. Using a mallet (or see the box on page 83), pound them to an even ½-inch thickness. Season on both sides with the salt and pepper.

Mince the garlic. In a medium skillet, heat the olive oil over medium-high heat. When the oil is shimmering, add the minced garlic and cook until fragrant, about 30 seconds. Add the chicken breasts and cook until golden brown and cooked through, 5 minutes on each side. Add the lemon juice and continue to cook for 1 minute more. Remove the chicken from the skillet and set aside to cool for 10 minutes. Then slice it into 1-inch-wide strips.

To make the dressing: Chop the scallions (both white and green parts). Mince the garlic. In a small bowl, whisk together the chopped scallion, minced garlic, dill, buttermilk, yogurt, mayonnaise, lemon juice, salt, and pepper.

To finish the salad: Coarsely chop the lettuce. Cut the ham into ¾-inch dice. Chop the plum tomatoes. Halve the avocado, remove the pit, and scoop out the flesh; then thinly slice. To assemble the salad, place the lettuce in a large bowl. Add the ham, tomatoes, avocado, chicken, and sliced egg. Serve with half the dressing on the side. Store extra dressing in an airtight container in the refrigerator for up to 5 days.

SERVING SIZE: 2¼ cups salad and 2 tablespoons dressing

NUTRITION INFORMATION (PER SERVING): Calories: 282; Total Fat: 16 grams; Saturated Fat: 3 grams; Protein: 25 grams; Total Carbohydrates: 12 grams; Sugars: 5 grams; Fiber: 5 grams; Cholesterol: 148 milligrams; Sodium: 575 milligrams

Tangy Buffalo-Style Salad with Chicken

This salad has the same flavors as Sunday Football-style buffalo wings for far fewer calories (those are usually around 100 per piece!). Both carrots and celery are incorporated in the salad, while the tangy dressing showcases the crumbled blue cheese—a little of the real thing goes a long way.

Prep time: 20 minutes, plus 30 minutes refrigeration *Cook time:* 10 minutes SERVES 4

1 pound boneless, skinless chicken breasts
¼ cup plus 1 tablespoon buffalo-flavored hot sauce (I like Frank's)
1 tablespoon canola oil
Cooking spray
½ cup nonfat plain Greek yogurt
1½ tablespoons white wine vinegar
3 tablespoons nonfat milk
1½ ounces blue cheese, crumbled (4½ tablespoons)
½ head romaine lettuce
4 medium celery ribs
2 medium carrots

Trim any visible fat from the chicken breasts and place the chicken between two pieces of plastic wrap. Pound to an even ½-inch thickness using a meat mallet (or see the box on page 83).

In a large bowl, combine the ¼ cup hot sauce and the canola oil. Add the chicken to the bowl, being sure to coat it evenly. Cover the bowl with plastic wrap and marinate in the refrigerator for at least 30 minutes or up to 8 hours.

Studies have found that visual cues aren't an accurate way to determine if chicken and meat are thoroughly cooked through. The best way is to insert a thermometer into the thickest part of the food. For chicken, you want to reach at least 165°F.

Preheat a grill or grill pan. Spray with cooking spray. Once the cooking spray is shimmering, add the chicken breasts, discarding the marinade. Cook the chicken until browned and cooked through, about 5 minutes on each side. Remove the chicken and set aside to cool for 10 minutes. Then brush the chicken with the remaining 1 tablespoon hot sauce. Cut the cooked chicken into bite-size pieces.

Place the yogurt, vinegar, milk, and half of the blue cheese in a blender or food processor. Blend until just combined, about 1 minute. Stir in the remaining blue cheese.

Tear the romaine lettuce into bite-size pieces; you should have about 8 cups. Cut the celery into ¼-inch-thick slices. Peel and grate the carrots. Toss the lettuce, celery, and carrots together in a large bowl; then add the dressing and toss to coat.

Divide the salad among four plates and top evenly with the chicken. Serve immediately.

SERVING SIZE: 3½ ounces chicken, 2½ cups salad, and 3 tablespoons dressing

NUTRITION INFORMATION (PER SERVING): Calories: 260; Total Fat: 10 grams; Saturated Fat: 3 grams; Protein: 32 grams; Total Carbohydrates: 11 grams; Sugars: 7 grams; Fiber: 3 grams; Cholesterol: 81 milligrams; Sodium: 704 milligrams

Soba Noodle Salad with Peanut Sauce

Soba noodles originate from Japan, where they symbolize longevity. Made from buckwheat, these noodles have a mild nutty flavor and are gluten-free. They are a perfect way to help you meet the USDA's recommendations for making half your daily grains whole grains. In addition, buckwheat contains the antioxidant rutin, which has been shown to help lower cholesterol.

Prep time: 15 minutes *Cook time:* 8 minutes SERVES 4

- 8 ounces soba (buckwheat) noodles
- 1 cup frozen shelled edamame
- 2 cloves garlic
- 3 tablespoons natural creamy peanut butter
- 1 tablespoon fresh lime juice
- 1 teaspoon fish sauce
- 1 teaspoon Sriracha sauce
- 3 tablespoons nonfat plain Greek yogurt
- 1 medium carrot
- ½ medium red bell pepper
- ½ English cucumber
- 1 scallion
- ¼ cup chopped fresh cilantro

Bring 4 quarts water to a boil in a large pot over high heat. When the water is boiling, add the soba noodles and cook for 5 minutes. Add the edamame and cook until the soba noodles are tender, about 3 minutes more. Drain the noodles and edamame in a colander and rinse under cold water. Place in a large bowl and set aside to cool.

Mince the garlic. In a large bowl, combine the minced garlic, ⅓ cup water, the peanut butter, lime juice, fish sauce, and Sriracha. Stir until smooth. Add the yogurt and stir until well combined. Add ½ cup of this peanut dressing to the soba noodles. Toss with tongs to coat evenly.

Forgo the expensive soba noodles found in health food markets. Instead, head to your local Asian market to purchase this whole grain noodle at a bargain price.

Peel and grate the carrot. Chop the red bell pepper, cucumber, and scallion (both white and green parts). Combine in a medium bowl.

Spoon ⅔ cup of dressed soba noodles into each of four bowls. Top each with ½ cup of the vegetable mixture, and then drizzle with

1 tablespoon of the remaining peanut dressing. Garnish each bowl with 1 tablespoon of the chopped cilantro.

SERVING SIZE: 1 bowl

NUTRITION INFORMATION (PER SERVING): Calories: 331; Total Fat: 8 grams; Saturated Fat: 1 gram; Protein: 17 grams; Total Carbohydrates: 53 grams; Sugars: 4 grams; Fiber: 3 grams; Cholesterol: 0 milligrams; Sodium: 626 milligrams

Speedy Lentil Soup

Weekdays are hectic, and slaving over a hot stove isn't always an option. This warming soup uses canned lentils to help speed up the cooking time while incorporating low-calorie parsley and cardamom to rev up the flavor.

Prep time: 15 minutes *Cook time:* 22 minutes

SERVES 4

- 7 sprigs fresh parsley
- 1 cup nonfat plain Greek yogurt
- 1 small onion
- 1 medium carrot, peeled
- 1 celery rib
- 1 cup packed fresh baby spinach
- 1 tablespoon extra-virgin olive oil
- 2 (15-ounce) cans brown lentils, drained and rinsed
- 1 (32-ounce) carton low-sodium chicken broth
- 2 bay leaves
- ⅛ teaspoon ground cardamom
- ½ teaspoon salt
- ⅛ teaspoon freshly ground black pepper

Chop the parsley leaves. In a small bowl, stir the parsley into the yogurt. Cover with plastic wrap and place in the refrigerator.

Chop the onion, carrot, and celery. Stack the spinach leaves, roll them up, and then slice into ribbons.

Heat the olive oil in a large pot over medium heat. When the oil is shimmering, add the onion, carrot, and celery, and cook until the onion is translucent, about 2 minutes. Add the lentils and stir to combine. Add the chicken broth and bay leaves. Turn the heat to high and bring to a boil. Then reduce the heat, cover the pot, and simmer until the lentils are tender, about 20 minutes.

Remove and discard the bay leaves. Stir in the cardamom, salt, pepper, and spinach. Place 1½ cups of the hot soup in each of four bowls. Just before serving, top each bowl with ¼ cup of the yogurt-parsley mixture.

To store fresh parsley, wrap it in a paper towel and place it in a resealable plastic bag. Refrigerate for up to 7 days.

SERVING SIZE: 1 bowl

NUTRITION INFORMATION (PER SERVING): Calories: 269; Total Fat: 4 grams; Saturated Fat: 1 gram; Protein: 22 grams; Total Carbohydrates: 35 grams; Sugars: 8 grams; Fiber: 16 grams; Cholesterol: 5 milligrams; Sodium: 710 milligrams

Black Bean Soup with Lime-Zested Yogurt Cream

Beans are a wonderful food to add to any healthy eating plan. They are chock-full of fiber and a good source of calcium, zinc, and iron along with the B vitamin folate, which is important for women who are pregnant or planning on becoming pregnant.

Prep time: 15 minutes *Cook time:* 37 minutes

SERVES 4

- 1 medium yellow onion
- ½ medium red bell pepper
- ½ medium green bell pepper
- 1 jalapeño pepper
- 4 cloves garlic
- 2 tablespoons olive oil
- 1 tablespoon ground cumin
- 2 teaspoons chili powder
- 2 (15-ounce) cans no-salt-added black beans, drained and rinsed
- 3 cups low-sodium chicken broth
- ½ teaspoon salt
- 1 lime
- 1 cup low-fat plain Greek yogurt

Peel and chop the onion. Chop the red and green bell peppers. Halve the jalapeño lengthwise, discard the seeds, and finely chop. Mince the garlic.

Heat the olive oil in a large saucepan over medium heat. When the oil is shimmering, add the onion, bell peppers, and jalapeño. Sauté until softened, 5 minutes. Add the minced garlic, cumin, and chili powder and cook, stirring continuously, for 2 minutes. Add the beans and chicken broth. Turn the heat to high and bring the mixture to a boil. Then lower the heat and simmer, uncovered, for 15 minutes.

Carefully pour half the soup into a large bowl, and using an immersion blender, puree until smooth, about 30 seconds. Stir the pureed soup back into the saucepan. Bring to a boil again; then lower the heat and simmer, uncovered, for 15 minutes, stirring occasionally. Add the salt and stir to incorporate.

While the soup is simmering, grate the zest from the lime and cut the lime into quarters. In a small bowl, stir together the lime zest and yogurt.

To keep sodium in check, always begin cooking with low-sodium ingredients like no-salt-added canned beans and low-sodium chicken broth. If needed, you can season with more salt at the end after tasting.

Ladle 1¼ cups of the soup into each of four bowls. Top each bowl with ¼ cup of the yogurt mixture and garnish with a lime wedge.

SERVING SIZE: 1 bowl

NUTRITION INFORMATION (PER SERVING): Calories: 323; Total Fat: 8 grams; Saturated Fat: 2 grams; Protein: 22 grams; Total Carbohydrates: 43 grams; Sugars: 6 grams; Fiber: 12 grams; Cholesterol: 3 milligrams; Sodium: 419 milligrams

Zucchini Soup

Root vegetables give this zucchini soup a flavorful punch and a hearty texture you are sure to love. My mom has been using these aromatic ingredients in her soups for years and now they have become a staple in mine.

Prep time: 35 minutes *Cook time:* 40 minutes SERVES 4

- 2 celery ribs
- 2 medium parsnips
- 1 medium turnip
- 1 medium onion
- 4 medium zucchini (about 1½ pounds)
- 2 tablespoons olive oil
- ½ teaspoon salt
- ¼ teaspoon freshly ground black pepper
- 4 cups low-sodium vegetable broth
- ¼ cup low-fat plain Greek yogurt
- ¼ cup whipped cream cheese
- 1 teaspoon grated lemon zest
- ¼ cup chopped fresh dill

Cut the celery into ½-inch dice. Peel and cut the parsnips and turnip into ½-inch dice. Chop the onion. Slice the zucchini into ½-inch-thick rounds.

In a large saucepan, heat the olive oil over medium heat. When the oil is shimmering, add the celery, parsnips, turnip, and onion and cook, stirring occasionally, until the vegetables have softened, 15 minutes. Add the zucchini, salt, and pepper and cook until the zucchini has softened slightly, 10 minutes. Add the vegetable broth, raise the heat, and bring to a boil. Then reduce the heat to medium-low and simmer until the zucchini is tender, about 15 minutes. Remove the saucepan from the heat and set aside to cool for about 15 minutes.

Meanwhile, in a medium bowl, stir together the yogurt, cream cheese, and lemon zest until well combined. Set aside.

Place the soup in a blender or food processor, and puree until smooth. Add the chopped dill and the yogurt mixture, and continue to blend until smooth and completely combined.

Spoon 1¾ cups of the soup into each of four bowls. Serve warm.

SERVING SIZE: 1 bowl

NUTRITION INFORMATION (PER SERVING): Calories: 208; Total Fat: 11 grams; Saturated Fat: 3 grams; Protein: 7 grams; Total Carbohydrates: 24 grams; Sugars: 14 grams; Fiber: 6 grams; Cholesterol: 11 milligrams; Sodium: 574 milligrams

Chunky Tomatillo Gazpacho

Combine fresh tomatillos with an array of crisp green vegetables to create a low-calorie, no-cook gazpacho, perfect for those steamy summer days. You can find fresh tomatillos at your local farmers market in July through September, while they are in peak season.

Prep time: 15 minutes, plus 1 hour refrigeration *Cook time:* 0 minutes SERVES 4

- 1 pound fresh tomatillos
- ½ English cucumber
- 3 scallions
- 1 medium green bell pepper
- 1 serrano chile
- 2 cloves garlic
- ¼ cup chopped fresh cilantro
- 1 cup low-sodium vegetable broth
- ¼ cup nonfat plain Greek yogurt
- 2 tablespoons fresh lime juice
- ½ teaspoon salt
- ¼ teaspoon freshly ground black pepper
- ½ red bell pepper

Husk the tomatillos and finely chop them. Finely chop the cucumber and scallions (both white and green parts). Slice the green bell pepper and the serrano chile in half, discard the seeds, and finely chop. Mince the garlic. In a large bowl, combine the chopped tomatillos, cucumber, scallions, bell pepper, chile, minced garlic, cilantro, vegetable broth, yogurt, lime juice, salt, and black pepper.

Place two-thirds of the mixture into a blender or food processor and blend until smooth. Pour the blended mixture back into the large bowl and stir to incorporate. Cover the bowl with plastic wrap and chill in the refrigerator for at least 1 hour, or up to 4 hours, to allow the flavors to combine.

To serve, ladle 1¼ cups of the gazpacho into each of four soup bowls. Finely chop the red bell pepper and garnish each bowl with 2 tablespoons. Serve cold.

SERVING SIZE: 1 bowl

NUTRITION INFORMATION (PER SERVING): Calories: 74; Total Fat: 1 gram; Saturated Fat: 0 grams; Protein: 4 grams; Total Carbohydrates: 14 grams; Sugars: 8 grams; Fiber: 4 grams; Cholesterol: 0 milligrams; Sodium: 342 milligrams

Chilled Tomato-Herb Soup

What's summer without a cold tomato soup? Nonfat plain Greek yogurt gives this soup a wonderful texture without using high-calorie heavy cream. Parsley, mint, and basil add even more flavor, leaving your taste buds begging for more.

Prep time: 20 minutes, plus 1 hour refrigeration *Cook time:* 0 minutes SERVES 4

- 4 scallions
- ½ cup fresh flat-leaf parsley leaves
- ½ cup fresh basil leaves
- ¼ cup fresh mint leaves, plus 4 leaves for garnish
- 1 (28-ounce) can peeled whole tomatoes, drained
- 2 tablespoons fresh lemon juice
- 2 teaspoons honey
- 1¾ cups nonfat plain Greek yogurt
- ¼ cup olive oil
- ½ teaspoon salt
- ½ teaspoon freshly ground black pepper

Chop the scallions, both white and green parts. Coarsely chop the parsley, basil, and ¼ cup of the mint leaves.

Place the herbs, scallions, tomatoes, lemon juice, and honey in a blender or food processor, and blend until smooth, about 45 seconds. Pour into a large serving bowl. Add 1½ cups of the yogurt, the olive oil, and the salt and pepper, and stir until well combined, smoothing any lumps with the back of the spoon. Cover the bowl with plastic wrap and place in the refrigerator to chill for at least 1 hour or up to 2 days.

Ladle 1¼ cups of the chilled soup into each of four bowls. Slice the remaining 4 mint leaves into strips. Top each bowl with 1 tablespoon of the remaining yogurt, and sprinkle with ½ tablespoon of the sliced mint.

SERVING SIZE: 1 bowl

NUTRITION INFORMATION (PER SERVING): Calories: 239; Total Fat: 14 grams; Saturated Fat: 2 grams; Protein: 12 grams; Total Carbohydrates: 18 grams; Sugars: 13 grams; Fiber: 3 grams; Cholesterol: 0 milligrams; Sodium: 772 milligrams

When they are available, use 2 pounds of fresh, seasonal tomatoes instead of canned. Peel, seed, and puree the tomatoes before adding them to your soup.

Avocado Soup with Pineapple Salsa

Venture into the world of avocados by making this creamy and oh-so-delicious soup! Topped with a pineapple salsa, it is a unique combination of flavors that work together magically.

Prep time: 20 minutes, plus 1 hour refrigeration *Cook time:* 0 minutes SERVES 4

FOR AVOCADO SOUP

3 medium avocados
2¾ cups low-sodium vegetable broth
¾ cup low-fat milk
½ cup low-fat plain Greek yogurt
2 tablespoons fresh lemon juice
¾ teaspoon salt
½ teaspoon freshly ground black pepper

FOR PINEAPPLE SALSA

1 fresh pineapple
¼ English cucumber, peeled
¼ medium red onion
½ jalapeño pepper
2 tablespoons chopped fresh cilantro
2 teaspoons fresh lime juice
⅛ teaspoon salt

To make the soup: Slice the avocados lengthwise, remove the pits, and scoop out the flesh, dropping it into the jar of a blender or food processor. Add the vegetable broth, milk, yogurt, lemon juice, salt, and pepper, and puree until smooth. Transfer to a bowl, cover with plastic wrap, and chill in the refrigerator for at least 1 hour or up to 4 hours.

While the soup is chilling, prepare the salsa: Slice the top off the pineapple, and then cut off all the skin. Quarter the pineapple lengthwise, remove the core, and refrigerate 3 of the quarters for another use. Cut the remaining quarter into ½-inch dice. Finely chop the cucumber and red onion. Halve the jalapeño lengthwise, discard the seeds, and finely chop. Place the pineapple, cucumber, onion, and jalapeño in a small bowl, and add the chopped cilantro, lime juice, and salt. Cover the bowl with plastic wrap and place in the refrigerator to marinate until the flavors are combined, at least 30 minutes and up to 1 hour.

To serve, ladle 1¼ cups of the soup into each of four soup bowls and top each bowl with ¼ cup of the pineapple salsa.

SERVING SIZE: 1 bowl

NUTRITION INFORMATION (PER SERVING): Calories: 244; Total Fat: 17 grams; Saturated Fat: 3 grams; Protein: 8 grams; Total Carbohydrates: 19 grams; Sugars: 8 grams; Fiber: 8 grams; Cholesterol: 3 milligrams; Sodium: 660 milligrams

Tuna and White Bean Salad on Rye Toast

This dressed-up tuna salad combines heart-healthy white cannellini beans with canned tuna. Instead of drowning these in high-fat mayonnaise, just a touch of light mayonnaise and nonfat plain Greek yogurt—along with other flavorful additions—gets the job done.

Prep time: 15 minutes *Cook time:* 0 minutes SERVES 8

- 1 (15-ounce) can no-salt-added cannellini beans
- 1 (5-ounce) can chunk light tuna packed in water
- ½ medium white onion
- 1 celery rib
- 2 tablespoons light mayonnaise
- 2 tablespoons nonfat plain Greek yogurt
- 1 tablespoon Dijon mustard
- 1 teaspoon fresh lemon juice
- 1 teaspoon chopped fresh parsley
- ¼ teaspoon salt
- ⅛ teaspoon freshly ground black pepper
- 2 medium tomatoes
- 16 slices seedless rye bread
- 8 green-leaf lettuce leaves

Drain and rinse the cannellini beans. Drain the canned tuna. Chop the onion and celery. In a medium bowl, using the back of a fork or a potato masher, mash together the beans, tuna, onion, and celery. Set aside.

In a small bowl, whisk together the mayonnaise, yogurt, mustard, lemon juice, parsley, salt, and pepper until well combined. Add the mayonnaise mixture to the tuna and stir to evenly coat.

Cut the tomatoes into about 16 thin slices. Toast the rye bread.

To assemble, on each of 8 slices of toast layer 1 leaf of lettuce, 2 slices of tomato, and ⅓ cup of the tuna and bean salad. Top each sandwich with a second slice of toast. Cut the sandwiches in half, and serve.

SERVING SIZE: 1 sandwich

NUTRITION INFORMATION (PER SERVING): Calories: 273; Total Fat: 4 grams; Saturated Fat: 0 grams; Protein: 15 grams; Total Carbohydrates: 43 grams; Sugars: 3 grams; Fiber: 5 grams; Cholesterol: 9 milligrams; Sodium: 562 milligrams

For everyday use, choose chunk light tuna packed in water. Chunk light is made from a smaller species of tuna that contains less mercury than the larger albacore.

Egg Salad Tea Sandwiches

My mom used to mash her egg salad, but I prefer using a hand blender to make it silky smooth. Now our big family debate is, whose tastes better?

Prep time: 40 minutes *Cook time:* 3 minutes SERVES 8

- 6 large eggs
- ¼ cup nonfat plain Greek yogurt
- ¼ cup light mayonnaise
- 1 tablespoon chopped fresh chives
- ½ teaspoon mustard powder
- ¼ teaspoon salt
- ¼ teaspoon freshly ground black pepper
- 4 large green-leaf lettuce leaves
- 8 slices 100% whole wheat bread

Place the eggs in a large pot and cover with cold water. Place the pot over high heat and bring to a boil; cook for 3 minutes. Then remove from the heat, cover the pot, and allow to stand for 15 minutes. Drain, and run cold water over the eggs until completely cool, about 10 minutes. Once they have cooled, peel the eggs and slice them in half lengthwise.

While the eggs are cooling, stir the yogurt, mayonnaise, chopped chives, mustard powder, salt, and pepper together in a medium bowl until well incorporated. Add the eggs to the yogurt mixture and use an immersion blender to puree until smooth.

Tear each lettuce leaf in half. To assemble the sandwiches, layer 2 pieces of lettuce on each of 4 slices of bread. Top each with ¼ cup of the egg salad. Cover with a second slice of bread. Using a serrated knife, carefully trim off the crust of each sandwich. Cut each sandwich in half, and serve.

SERVING SIZE: 1 tea sandwich

NUTRITION INFORMATION (PER SERVING): Calories: 153; Total Fat: 7 grams; Saturated Fat: 2 grams; Protein: 9 grams; Total Carbohydrates: 13 grams; Sugars: 2 grams; Fiber: 2 grams; Cholesterol: 142 milligrams; Sodium: 315 milligrams

When choosing eggs, size matters but color does not. There is no nutritional difference between white and brown varieties—the color of the shell has simply to do with the hen's earlobes. Hens with white earlobes lay white eggs, while those with red earlobes lay brown ones.

Lighter Lobster Rolls

A traditional lobster roll averages around 1,020 calories and 66 grams of fat from gobs of mayo and butter. You can get the same flavor with simple swaps—and you'll save more than 600 calories and 50 grams of fat!

Prep time: 15 minutes *Cook time*: 0 minutes

SERVES 4

- 1 medium celery rib
- 2 tablespoons chopped fresh chives
- 3 tablespoons nonfat plain Greek yogurt
- 3 tablespoons light mayonnaise
- 2 tablespoons fresh lemon juice
- ¼ teaspoon salt
- ⅛ teaspoon freshly ground black pepper
- 1 pound cooked lobster meat
- 4 (100% whole wheat) hotdog rolls
- 8 teaspoons unsalted butter, at room temperature
- 4 lemon wedges

Finely chop the celery. In a medium bowl, stir the chopped celery, chives, yogurt, mayonnaise, lemon juice, salt, and pepper to thoroughly combine. Cut the lobster meat into small chunks and fold it into the mixture until well incorporated.

Split open each hotdog roll and toast it. Spread 2 teaspoons of the butter inside each roll, and then spoon in ⅔ cup of the lobster mixture.

Garnish each lobster roll with a lemon wedge, and serve immediately.

SERVING SIZE: 1 lobster roll

NUTRITION INFORMATION (PER SERVING): Calories: 391; Total Fat: 15 grams; Saturated Fat: 7 grams; Protein: 35 grams; Total Carbohydrates: 28 grams; Sugars: 5 grams; Fiber: 4 grams; Cholesterol: 126 milligrams; Sodium: 665 milligrams

If you want to forgo cooking your own lobster, look for freshly cooked lobster meat at your local fish market or at the fish counter at your grocery store. Some markets will also steam fresh lobster for you upon request.

Caprese Panini

The classic version of this sandwich uses a high-fat pesto sauce—half a cup has about 300 calories and 28 grams of fat. Here we slash that to just 120 calories and 14 grams of fat.

Prep time: 5 minutes *Cook time:* 12 minutes SERVES 4

Cooking spray
¼ cup store-bought pesto sauce
¼ cup nonfat plain Greek yogurt
1 (14½-ounce) whole-grain ciabatta
12 fresh basil leaves
1 medium tomato, thinly sliced
4 ounces fresh mozzarella cheese, cut into four ½-inch-thick slices

Coat a panini press or a grill pan with cooking spray, and heat it over medium heat.

In a small bowl, stir together the pesto and yogurt. Set aside.

Slice the ciabatta into four 5-inch-long pieces, and then slice each piece in half lengthwise to create a sandwich roll. Place the bottom side of the rolls on a clean work surface and split open. Spread 1 tablespoon of the pesto mixture over the bottom of each roll, and then add 3 basil leaves, 2 to 3 slices of tomato, and 1 slice of mozzarella. Cover each sandwich with the top side of the roll.

Place the sandwiches, one at a time, in the heated panini press or grill pan. Cook until the bread is golden brown and the cheese has melted, about 3 minutes. (If using a grill pan, place a second heavy pan over the sandwich to press it, and turn once to cook both sides.) Serve warm.

SERVING SIZE: 1 sandwich

NUTRITION INFORMATION (PER SERVING): Calories: 369; Total Fat: 14 grams; Saturated Fat: 4 grams; Protein: 17 grams; Total Carbohydrates: 42 grams; Sugars: 2 grams; Fiber: 4 grams; Cholesterol: 19 milligrams; Sodium: 636 milligrams

Roasted Eggplant and Chickpea-Stuffed Pitas

Each summer I visit my in-laws in Israel and we always eat at the same barbecue joint. At the beginning of the meal, the waiter brings out about ten tapas, including roasted chickpeas, fried eggplant, pickled vegetables, cabbage slaw, tahini, and olives. We eat these delicious dishes with warmed pita bread on the side. I was inspired to combine a few of these flavors into one stuffed pita here!

Prep time: 15 minutes *Cook time:* 35 minutes SERVES 4

- 4 (6½-inch) whole wheat pitas
- ¾ medium eggplant (12 ounces)
- 3 tablespoons olive oil
- ½ teaspoon salt
- ¼ teaspoon freshly ground black pepper
- 1 small yellow onion
- 2 cloves garlic
- 1 medium red bell pepper
- 1 (15-ounce) can no-salt-added chickpeas
- 2 tablespoons chopped fresh parsley
- 2 tablespoons chopped fresh mint
- ½ cup nonfat plain Greek yogurt

Preheat the oven to 400°F.

Using a serrated knife, slice ½ inch off the top of each pita. Discard the tops or save them for another use.

Cut the eggplant into eight ¼-inch-thick rounds. In a small bowl, whisk together 2 tablespoons of the olive oil, ¼ teaspoon of the salt, and ⅛ teaspoon of the black pepper. Brush this mixture over both sides of the eggplant slices, and arrange them in an even layer on a baking sheet. Roast, turning them over halfway through, until soft and golden brown, 25 minutes.

Meanwhile, chop the onion. Mince the garlic. Slice the red bell pepper in half, discard the seeds, and cut into ½-inch dice. Drain and rinse the chickpeas. In a medium saucepan, heat the remaining 1 tablespoon olive oil over medium heat. When the oil is shimmering, add the chopped onion and cook until softened and translucent, 2 minutes. Add the minced garlic and cook until fragrant, 30 seconds. Add the diced bell pepper and cook until softened, about 2 minutes. Add the chickpeas, remaining ¼ teaspoon salt, and remaining

⅛ teaspoon black pepper. Continue cooking over medium heat until warmed through, 5 minutes. Remove the pan from the heat and set it aside.

In a medium bowl, combine the parsley and mint with the yogurt.

To assemble, stuff 2 eggplant slices into each pita. Add 1 tablespoon of the yogurt mixture, then ¾ cup of the chickpea mixture, and top with an additional 1 tablespoon of the yogurt mixture.

SERVING SIZE: 1 stuffed pita

NUTRITION INFORMATION (PER SERVING): Calories: 412; Total Fat: 13 grams; Saturated Fat: 2 grams; Protein: 16 grams; Total Carbohydrates: 62 grams; Sugars: 6 grams; Fiber: 13 grams; Cholesterol: 0 milligrams; Sodium: 656 milligrams

Grilled Vegetable Wrap with Herbed Cheese

When I was a teenager, my parents owned a cheese store on Chambers Street in New York City, where they sold more than four hundred varieties of cheese. When the busy season arrived, I was asked to help out. During lunch, I loved trying new varieties in my sandwich. One of my favorites was an herbed cheese, which was my inspiration for this wrap.

Prep time: 15 minutes, plus 1 hour refrigeration *Cook time:* 10 minutes SERVES 4

- 1 tablespoon balsamic vinegar
- 1 tablespoon honey
- ¼ teaspoon salt
- 3 tablespoons olive oil
- ½ red bell pepper, cut into ½-inch-wide strips
- 1 medium zucchini, cut into ½-inch-wide strips
- 1 portobello mushroom cap, cut into ½-inch-wide strips
- Cooking spray
- ⅓ cup soft garlic-and-herb cheese (I like Boursin)
- ¼ cup nonfat plain Greek yogurt
- 4 (8-inch) 100% whole wheat tortillas

In a medium bowl, whisk together the vinegar, honey, and salt. Slowly drizzle in the olive oil, continuing to whisk until emulsified. Add the red bell pepper, zucchini, and mushroom to the bowl and toss to evenly coat. Cover with plastic wrap and place in the refrigerator to marinate for at least 1 hour and as long as 2 hours.

Coat a grill pan with cooking spray. Place it over medium heat.

In a small bowl, combine the cheese and yogurt. Set aside.

Warm the tortillas on the grill pan, about 1 minute per side, and then set one on each of four plates.

Pour off the extra marinade, and add the red pepper, zucchini, and mushroom strips to the hot grill pan. Cook, stirring occasionally, until the vegetables are tender and their edges are lightly browned, 10 minutes. Remove the pan from the heat and set aside to cool slightly.

Spread 2 tablespoons of the cheese mixture over each tortilla. Divide the grilled vegetables evenly among the tortillas, and then roll up each wrap. Serve warm.

SERVING SIZE: 1 wrap

NUTRITION INFORMATION (PER SERVING): Calories: 299; Total Fat: 20 grams; Saturated Fat: 7 grams; Protein: 8 grams; Total Carbohydrates: 26 grams; Sugars: 8 grams; Fiber: 5 grams; Cholesterol: 18 milligrams; Sodium: 554 milligrams

CHAPTER 5

Main Dishes

Grilled Asian Shrimp Skewers with Dipping Sauce

In these Asian-inspired shrimp skewers, Greek yogurt is combined with garlic, lime zest, and black pepper for a flavorful marinade.

Prep time: 15 minutes, plus 1 hour refrigeration *Cook time:* 2 minutes SERVES 4

- 2 cloves garlic
- 1½ cups nonfat plain Greek yogurt
- Grated zest and juice of 1 lime
- ¼ teaspoon freshly ground black pepper
- 1 pound (about 32) extra-large shrimp, peeled and deveined
- 1 teaspoon reduced-sodium soy sauce
- 1 teaspoon fish sauce
- 1 teaspoon light brown sugar
- ½ teaspoon Sriracha sauce
- 2 tablespoons chopped fresh cilantro

Mince 1 clove of the garlic. In a medium bowl, combine ½ cup of the yogurt with the minced garlic, lime zest, and pepper. Add the shrimp and toss to coat evenly. Cover with plastic wrap and allow to marinate in the refrigerator for exactly 1 hour.

Meanwhile, preheat the grill for medium heat. If you are using wooden skewers, soak them in water for at least 10 minutes.

Prepare the dipping sauce: Mince the remaining garlic clove. In a medium bowl, whisk together the minced garlic, lime juice, soy sauce, fish sauce, brown sugar, and Sriracha until the sugar is completely dissolved. Add the remaining 1 cup yogurt and stir until smooth. Top with the chopped cilantro.

Remove the shrimp from the marinade and allow the excess to drip off. Remove the skewers from the water and thread 4 shrimp onto each skewer. Grill until the shrimp are pink and cooked through, turning them over once, 1 to 2 minutes. Serve warm, with the dipping sauce alongside.

SERVING SIZE: 2 shrimp skewers and ¼ cup dipping sauce

NUTRITION INFORMATION (PER SERVING): Calories: 131; Total Fat: 1 gram; Saturated Fat: 0 grams; Protein: 23 grams; Total Carbohydrates: 6 grams; Sugars: 4 grams; Fiber: 0 grams; Cholesterol: 143 milligrams; Sodium: 810 milligrams

After marinating the shrimp, discard any remaining marinade and wash any dishes that were used. Doing so will help prevent any risk of food-borne illness.

Grilled Flounder with Avocado Sauce

This perfect weeknight dish can be whipped up in less than thirty minutes. The simple, silky avocado sauce complements the flaky white fish beautifully.

Prep time: 20 minutes *Cook time:* 6 minutes

SERVES 4

- 2 tablespoons canola oil
- 1 teaspoon ground cumin
- ⅛ teaspoon salt
- ⅛ teaspoon freshly ground black pepper
- 4 (5-ounce) flounder fillets
- 1 clove garlic
- ½ Hass avocado
- 2 tablespoons chopped fresh cilantro leaves, plus whole leaves for garnish
- ½ cup nonfat plain Greek yogurt
- 2 teaspoons green hot sauce (I like Tabasco)
- 1 tablespoon fresh lime juice
- 3 tablespoons whole milk

Preheat a grill to medium-high, or place a grill pan over medium-high heat.

In a medium bowl, whisk together the canola oil, cumin, salt, and pepper. Brush this mixture over both sides of the fish fillets and set aside.

Mince the garlic. Place the avocado flesh, minced garlic, chopped cilantro leaves, yogurt, hot sauce, and lime juice in a blender or food processor, and puree until smooth. Add the milk and blend until well incorporated. Set aside.

Grill the flounder until it is opaque, about 3 minutes per side. Top each piece of fish with ½ cup of the avocado sauce. Garnish with the whole cilantro leaves, and serve.

SERVING SIZE: 1 piece flounder and ½ cup avocado sauce

NUTRITION INFORMATION (PER SERVING): Calories: 309; Total Fat: 22 grams; Saturated Fat: 3 grams; Protein: 25 grams; Total Carbohydrates: 5 grams; Sugars: 2 grams; Fiber: 2 grams; Cholesterol: 80 milligrams; Sodium: 678 milligrams

rilled Asian Shrimp Skewers
ith Dipping Sauce (page 129)

Roasted Salmon with Dill-Yogurt Sauce
and Creamed Spinach (page 133)

Turkey Tacos with Pico de Gallo and Crema Mexicana (page 135)

Lamb Kebobs with Mint-Yogurt Sauce (page 143)

Crunchy Buttermilk Chicken Fingers with Honey-Mustard Dipping Sauce (page 139)

Spaghetti Carbonara with Peas (page 151)

White Margherita Pizza (page 155)

Potato Salad with Parsnips and Edamame (page 186)

Artichoke, Fennel, and
Ricotta–Stuffed Shells (page 160)

Pasta Salad with Tomatoes, Peppers, and Olives (page 188)

Rosemary Olive Bread (page 190)

Vanilla-Lover Cupcakes (page 208)

Ice Cream Sandwiches with Pomegranate (page 218)

Chocolate-Hazelnut Pudding Shooters (page 224)

Peanut Butter–Banana
Ice Box Bars (page 219)

Light and Dark Chocolate Brownies (page 220)

Crispy Fish with Tartar Sauce and Kale Chips

When I was in college, we used to order fish sandwiches instead of burgers and pizza—we thought it was a healthier choice. As I took more nutrition courses and restaurants began to unveil their calorie counts, I was sorely disappointed! In order to satisfy my craving for fish and chips, I now make my own crispy baked fish using homemade whole wheat breadcrumbs and a lighter tartar sauce made with low-fat Greek yogurt. With kale chips on the side, it is indeed a healthier choice!

Prep time: 35 minutes *Cook time:* 45 minutes SERVES 4

FOR TARTAR SAUCE

¼ shallot

1 teaspoon capers

¼ cup light mayonnaise

¼ cup low-fat plain Greek yogurt

1 tablespoon white wine vinegar

1 teaspoon Dijon mustard

⅛ teaspoon kosher salt

⅛ teaspoon freshly ground black pepper

FOR CRISPY FISH

4 slices whole wheat bread

Cooking spray

4 (5-ounce) flounder fillets or other white flaky fish

⅛ teaspoon freshly ground black pepper

2 large eggs

2 large egg whites

½ teaspoon Cajun seasoning

FOR KALE CHIPS

1 tablespoon olive oil

⅛ teaspoon kosher salt

¼ teaspoon freshly ground black pepper

½ bunch (4 ounces) fresh kale, preferably dinosaur (lacinato) kale, cut into 1-inch pieces

Preheat the oven to 375°F.

To prepare the tartar sauce: Chop the shallot and capers. Combine the shallot, capers, mayonnaise, yogurt, vinegar, mustard, salt, and pepper in a medium bowl. Cover with plastic wrap and refrigerate until ready to use.

To prepare the fish: Using clean hands, tear the slices of whole wheat bread into small pieces. Place them in a food processor and pulse until fine crumbs form, about 30 seconds. Sprinkle the crumbs over a dry baking sheet and toast in the oven until lightly browned, about 10 minutes. Remove from the oven and set aside to cool slightly. Keep the oven at 375°F. Coat a baking sheet with cooking spray and set it aside.

Season the fish on both sides with the pepper. In a medium bowl, whisk together the eggs and egg whites. In a shallow dish or large plate, combine the Cajun seasoning with the breadcrumbs.

Dip 1 piece of fish in the egg mixture, then dredge it in the breadcrumb mixture. Dip the same piece of fish back in the egg mixture, then dredge again in the breadcrumb mixture, this time pressing down firmly to be sure the crumbs adhere all over the fish. Place the coated fish on the prepared baking sheet. Repeat with the remaining 3 pieces of fish. Bake the fish until crispy and lightly browned, about 20 minutes. Then remove the baking sheet from the oven and place the fish on a platter. Cover with aluminum foil to keep warm and set it aside. Raise the oven temperature to 400°F for the kale chips.

To prepare the kale chips: Whisk the olive oil, salt, and pepper together in a large bowl. Add the chopped kale and toss until well coated. Place the kale in an even layer on the same baking sheet used for the breadcrumbs and bake until crisp, about 10 minutes.

Place one fish fillet on each of four plates and top with 2 tablespoons of the tartar sauce. Serve the kale chips alongside.

SERVING SIZE: 1 piece fish, 2 tablespoons tartar sauce, and ½ cup kale chips

NUTRITION INFORMATION: Calories: 321; Total Fat: 15 grams; Saturated Fat: 3 grams; Protein: 29 grams; Total Carbohydrates: 17 grams; Sugars: 3 grams; Fiber: 3 grams; Cholesterol: 164 milligrams; Sodium: 989 milligrams

Look for kale with deeply colored green leaves—and avoid leaves that look wilted, limp, dry, or have signs of insect damage. Store it unwashed, wrapped in a moist paper towel, in a plastic bag in the refrigerator for up to 3 days.

Roasted Salmon with Dill-Yogurt Sauce and Creamed Spinach

This gorgeous weeknight dinner can be whipped up in no time. The unbelievably rich flavors make it seem almost impossible that it contains fewer than 300 calories per serving.

Prep time: 20 minutes *Cook time:* 25 minutes SERVES 4

FOR SALMON

Cooking spray

2 lemons

4 (6-ounce) salmon fillets

⅛ teaspoon salt

⅛ teaspoon freshly ground black pepper

FOR DILL-YOGURT SAUCE

¼ shallot

1 tablespoon capers

1 tablespoon chopped fresh dill

6 tablespoons nonfat plain Greek yogurt

1 teaspoon fresh lemon juice

1 tablespoon nonfat milk

FOR CREAMED SPINACH

10 ounces fresh or frozen spinach (thawed and well drained if frozen)

1 clove garlic

1 teaspoon canola oil

¼ cup nonfat plain Greek yogurt

Preheat the oven to 400°F. Coat a baking sheet with cooking spray and set it aside.

Cut the lemons into ¼-inch-thick rounds. Season both sides of the salmon with the salt and pepper, and place the fillets skin-side down on the prepared baking sheet, spacing them about 1½ inches apart. Arrange the lemon slices over the salmon. Place the baking sheet on the top rack in the oven and cook until the fish is opaque and flakes easily with a fork, about 20 minutes.

While the salmon roasts, prepare the dill-yogurt sauce: Finely mince the shallot. Drain and chop the capers. Combine the shallot, dill, capers, yogurt, lemon juice, and milk in a small bowl. Stir until well incorporated.

To prepare the creamed spinach, chop the spinach and mince the garlic. Heat the canola oil in a large skillet over medium heat. When the oil is shimmering, add the minced garlic and sauté gently until fragrant, about 1 minute. Add the chopped spinach and cook until just wilted and warmed through, 3 to 4 minutes. Remove from the heat, spoon the yogurt over the spinach, and gently stir it in.

Place one piece of salmon on each of four plates. Spoon ½ cup of the creamed spinach and 2 tablespoons of the dill-yogurt sauce on either side of the salmon. Serve immediately.

SERVING SIZE: 1 salmon fillet, ½ cup creamed spinach, and 2 tablespoons dill-yogurt sauce

NUTRITION INFORMATION (PER SERVING): Calories: 297; Total Fat: 12 grams; Saturated Fat: 2 grams; Protein: 40 grams; Total Carbohydrates: 6 grams; Sugars: 2 grams; Fiber: 2 grams; Cholesterol: 94 milligrams; Sodium: 281 milligrams

Turkey Tacos with Pico de Gallo and Crema Mexicana

My son adores taco night. I make his favorite meal before he leaves for sleepaway camp and on those days when he needs a little extra TLC. With so much nutritional goodness, this is one dish I am always delighted to cook upon request.

Prep time: 25 minutes *Cook time:* 20 minutes

SERVES 4

FOR TACOS

2 cloves garlic
1 jalapeño pepper
2 tablespoons olive oil
1 teaspoon chili powder
½ teaspoon ground cumin
1 pound lean ground turkey
¾ cup canned no-salt-added diced tomatoes
¼ teaspoon salt
⅛ teaspoon freshly ground black pepper
Cooking spray
8 (6-inch) corn tortillas
1 cup shredded romaine lettuce
1 cup reduced-fat shredded Mexican cheese blend

FOR PICO DE GALLO

1 medium tomato, diced
½ medium white onion, diced
½ jalapeño pepper, finely diced
2 cloves garlic, minced
2 tablespoons fresh lime juice
2 tablespoons chopped fresh cilantro
¼ teaspoon salt

FOR CREMA MEXICANA

1 cup nonfat plain Greek yogurt
2 teaspoons grated lime zest
1 tablespoon fresh lime juice
¼ teaspoon salt
⅛ teaspoon hot sauce

Mince the garlic. Halve the jalapeño lengthwise, discard the seeds, and finely dice. Heat the olive oil in a large sauté pan over medium heat. When the oil is shimmering, add the minced garlic, diced jalapeño, chili powder, and cumin. Sauté until the garlic and jalapeño have softened, about 1 minute. Add the ground turkey and break it up in the pan, using a spoon. Cook until well browned, about 4 minutes.

To make 1 cup of your own reduced-fat Mexican cheese blend, shred 2 ounces each of reduced-fat Monterey Jack and reduced-fat cheddar cheese.

Add the tomatoes, salt, and black pepper. Turn the heat to low and simmer until most of the liquid from the tomatoes has evaporated, about 5 minutes.

Meanwhile, make the pico de gallo: In a small bowl, stir together the tomato, onion, jalapeño, garlic, lime juice, cilantro, and salt until well incorporated. Set aside.

To make the crema mexicana: Stir together the yogurt, lime zest and juice, salt, and hot sauce in a small bowl until well incorporated.

Heat a skillet over medium-low heat. Spray the skillet with cooking spray. Warm the corn tortillas, one at a time, for 30 seconds on each side. Place 2 tortillas on each of four plates. Spoon 6 tablespoons of the turkey mixture over each warmed tortilla. Top with 3 tablespoons of the pico de gallo and 2 tablespoons each of the crema mexicana, lettuce, and shredded Mexican cheese blend. Fold together and enjoy.

SERVING SIZE: 2 filled tacos

NUTRITION INFORMATION (PER SERVING): Calories: 436; Total Fat: 21 grams; Saturated Fat: 6 grams; Protein: 37 grams; Total Carbohydrates: 28 grams; Sugars: 6 grams; Fiber: 5 grams; Cholesterol: 89 milligrams; Sodium: 765 milligrams

Chicken with Mushroom Sauce

After having three kids, my husband and I made it a point to go out every Saturday night for date night. But every time we had Italian, my husband would order mushrooms and chicken in a cream sauce—a very high-calorie meal! To satisfy his cravings at home, I created this healthier dish.

Prep time: 12 minutes *Cook time:* 30 minutes SERVES 4

- 4 (6-ounce) boneless, skinless chicken breast cutlets
- ½ teaspoon salt
- ¼ teaspoon freshly ground black pepper
- 2 tablespoons canola oil
- 1 shallot, minced
- 2 cloves garlic, minced
- 6 cups (about 1 pound) cremini mushrooms, sliced
- 3 tablespoons unbleached all-purpose flour
- 1 cup reduced-sodium chicken broth
- ½ cup dry white wine
- 1 teaspoon chopped fresh thyme leaves
- ⅔ cup low-fat plain Greek yogurt
- 2 tablespoons chopped fresh parsley leaves

Season the chicken breasts on both sides with ¼ teaspoon of the salt and the pepper. Heat the oil in a large skillet over medium heat. When the oil is shimmering, add the chicken and cook until browned, about 6 minutes on each side. Transfer the chicken to a plate and set it aside.

Add the shallot and garlic to the skillet you used for the chicken, and cook over medium heat until fragrant, about 1 minute. Add the cremini mushrooms and continue to cook, stirring occasionally, until the mushrooms have softened and their juices are released, about 8 minutes. Sprinkle the flour over the mushroom mixture and continue cooking, still stirring, until it is incorporated, about 1 minute. Add the broth, wine, and remaining ¼ teaspoon salt, and bring to a boil. Lower the heat to a simmer and continue to cook until the sauce thickens, 2 minutes. Add the chicken and thyme to the skillet and simmer gently over medium-low heat for 4 minutes. Remove the skillet from the heat.

Place the yogurt in a small bowl. Spoon ¼ cup of the mushroom sauce into the yogurt to warm it. Add the warmed yogurt mixture to the skillet and stir to incorporate. Place 1 piece of chicken on each of four plates and top with ¾ cup of the mushroom sauce. Sprinkle the parsley over the chicken, and serve immediately.

SERVING SIZE: 1 piece chicken and ¾ cup sauce

NUTRITION INFORMATION (PER SERVING): Calories: 335; Total Fat: 12 grams; Saturated Fat: 2 grams; Protein: 45 grams; Total Carbohydrates: 11 grams; Sugars: 4 grams; Fiber: 1 gram; Cholesterol: 109 milligrams; Sodium: 532 milligrams

Crunchy Buttermilk Chicken Fingers with Honey-Mustard Dipping Sauce

A combination of nonfat Greek yogurt and low-fat buttermilk is used here as a lower-calorie substitute for regular buttermilk. Dredged in a combination of flour and whole wheat panko breadcrumbs for crunch, this version of the classic favorite will have both adults and kids begging for more.

Prep time: 20 minutes *Cook time:* 30 minutes SERVES 4

FOR CHICKEN FINGERS

Cooking spray
2⁄3 cup nonfat plain Greek yogurt
1⁄3 cup low-fat buttermilk
1 cup whole wheat panko breadcrumbs
1⁄2 cup unbleached all-purpose flour
1⁄2 cup whole wheat flour
1⁄4 cup cornmeal
1 teaspoon onion powder
1 teaspoon garlic powder
1⁄4 teaspoon paprika
1 1⁄4 pounds chicken breast tenders
1⁄4 teaspoon salt
1⁄4 teaspoon freshly ground black pepper

FOR DIPPING SAUCE

6 tablespoons nonfat plain Greek yogurt
2 tablespoons Dijon mustard
2 tablespoons honey

To prepare the chicken fingers: Preheat the oven to 375°F. Coat a baking sheet with cooking spray and set it aside.

In a large bowl, whisk together the yogurt and buttermilk. In another large bowl, mix together the panko, all-purpose flour, whole wheat flour, cornmeal, onion powder, garlic powder, and paprika. Set aside.

Season the chicken on both sides with the salt and pepper. Dip each chicken tender in the yogurt mixture, allowing the excess to drip off. Then dredge in the panko mixture, pressing with your fingertips to evenly coat both sides. Place the tenders on the prepared baking sheet, leaving about 1 1⁄2 inches between them. Bake until the chicken is browned, about 30 minutes.

Meanwhile, make the dipping sauce: Combine the yogurt, mustard, and honey in a small bowl.

Place 3 chicken fingers on each of four plates, and serve with 2 tablespoons dipping sauce on the side.

SERVING SIZE: 3 chicken fingers and 2 tablespoons dipping sauce

NUTRITION INFORMATION (PER SERVING): Calories: 330; Total Fat: 4 grams; Saturated Fat: 1 gram; Protein: 39 grams; Total Carbohydrates: 33 grams; Sugars: 11 grams; Fiber: 2 grams; Cholesterol: 92 milligrams; Sodium: 547 milligrams

Greek-Style Chicken with Olives, Tomatoes, and Feta

The flavors of olives, tomatoes, and feta meld beautifully in this Mediterranean-inspired dish. Serve it with a freshly baked whole-grain baguette or over whole wheat couscous.

Prep time: 10 minutes *Cook time:* 45 minutes SERVES 4

- 1¼ pounds boneless, skinless chicken thighs
- ¼ teaspoon kosher salt
- ⅛ teaspoon freshly ground black pepper
- 1 tablespoon olive oil
- 1 medium yellow onion, chopped
- 2 cloves garlic, minced
- ⅓ cup dry white wine
- ¾ cup pitted kalamata olives, chopped
- 2 (14.5-ounce) cans no-salt-added diced tomatoes
- 2 teaspoons dried oregano
- ⅛ teaspoon paprika
- 2 ounces feta cheese, crumbled (6 tablespoons; I like goat's-milk feta)
- 2 tablespoons low-fat plain Greek yogurt

Trim the fat off the chicken and cut the meat into 2-inch pieces. Season the chicken on both sides with ⅛ teaspoon each of the salt and the pepper. Heat the olive oil in a large skillet over medium heat. When the oil is shimmering, add the chicken and cook until it is browned, about 8 minutes. Remove the chicken from the skillet and set it aside.

Add the chopped onion to the same skillet, still over medium heat, and cook until soft and translucent, about 3 minutes. Add the minced garlic and cook until fragrant, 30 seconds. Stir in the wine and cook until it has reduced by half, about 2 minutes. Add the chopped olives, tomatoes, oregano, paprika, and remaining ⅛ teaspoon salt, and stir to incorporate. Raise the heat to high and bring the mixture to a boil. Then reduce the heat to low and simmer until the tomatoes and olives begin to soften, about 5 minutes.

Return the browned chicken to the skillet and toss to coat. Continue to simmer over low heat, covered, until the chicken is cooked through, 20 to 25 minutes. Then stir in the feta and cook for 2 minutes more.

Remove the skillet from the heat and allow to cool for 1 minute. Gently stir in the yogurt until incorporated. Spoon 1¾ cups of the chicken mixture onto each of four plates. Serve warm.

SERVING SIZE: 1¾ cups

NUTRITION INFORMATION (PER SERVING): Calories: 350; Total Fat: 15 grams; Saturated Fat: 5 grams; Protein: 33 grams; Total Carbohydrates: 15 grams; Sugars: 9 grams; Fiber: 2 grams; Cholesterol: 135 milligrams; Sodium: 584 milligrams

Lamb Kebobs with Mint-Yogurt Sauce

Lean cuts of lamb can be a part of a well-rounded eating plan. The leg, loin, and rack are good choices, delivering 23 grams of protein and 175 calories for every 3 ounces. Lamb is an excellent source of vitamin B_{12}, niacin, selenium, and zinc and a good source of riboflavin and iron. I make these lamb kebobs for a quick meal, and love how fabulous they taste.

Prep time: 25 minutes, plus 1 hour refrigeration *Cook time:* 12 minutes SERVES 4

- 4 cloves garlic
- 1½ pounds lamb tenderloin
- ¾ cup chopped fresh mint leaves
- 1 cup nonfat plain Greek yogurt
- 2 tablespoons dry white wine
- ¼ teaspoon salt
- ¼ teaspoon freshly ground black pepper
- 4 shallots
- 1 medium green bell pepper
- 16 cherry tomatoes

Crush 3 of the garlic cloves. Trim the fat off the lamb and cut the meat into 1-inch cubes. In a medium bowl, whisk together ½ cup of the chopped mint, the crushed garlic, ½ cup of the yogurt, the wine, ⅛ teaspoon of the salt, and ⅛ teaspoon of the pepper. Add the lamb cubes and toss to coat evenly. Cover the bowl with plastic wrap and set in the refrigerator to marinate for exactly 1 hour.

If you are using wooden skewers, soak them in water for at least 10 minutes.

Slice each shallot into 4 large chunks. Cut the bell pepper in half, discard the seeds, and cut into 2-inch pieces.

Preheat a grill or a grill pan over medium-high heat.

Remove the lamb from the marinade, allowing the excess to drip off. (Discard the marinade.) Thread each skewer with 2 to 3 pieces of the lamb, 2 pieces of shallot, 2 tomatoes, and 2 pieces of bell pepper. Grill the kebobs, turning them several times, until the lamb is browned and cooked through, 12 minutes.

Meanwhile, make the mint-yogurt sauce: Mince the remaining clove of garlic. In a small bowl, whisk together the remaining ¼ cup chopped mint, the minced garlic, the remaining ½ cup yogurt, and the remaining ⅛ teaspoon salt and pepper until thoroughly combined.

Set 2 lamb skewers on each of four plates and place 2 tablespoons of the mint-yogurt sauce on the side.

SERVING SIZE: 2 lamb skewers and 2 tablespoons sauce

NUTRITION INFORMATION (PER SERVING): Calories: 310; Total Fat: 9 grams; Saturated Fat: 3 grams; Protein: 42 grams; Total Carbohydrates: 15 grams; Sugars: 5 grams; Fiber: 2 grams; Cholesterol: 109 milligrams; Sodium: 266 milligrams

Beef Stroganoff

High-calorie versions of this recipe use butter, sour cream, and cream of mushroom soup to give it body. To lighten it up, my recipe uses low-sodium beef broth and red wine for a yummy flavor and Greek yogurt for a creamy texture. I like to serve it over whole wheat egg noodles.

Prep time: 15 minutes *Cook time:* 20 minutes SERVES 4

- 1¼ pounds flank steak
- 1 medium yellow onion
- 10 ounces button mushrooms
- 2 cloves garlic
- 2 tablespoons canola oil
- 3 tablespoons unbleached all-purpose flour
- 1 cup low-sodium beef broth
- ½ cup dry red wine
- ¼ teaspoon salt
- ¼ teaspoon freshly ground black pepper
- ⅔ cup low-fat plain Greek yogurt

Cut the flank steak into 1-inch cubes. Cut the onion into ½-inch dice. Slice the mushrooms. Mince the garlic.

Heat the canola oil in a large skillet over medium heat. When the oil is shimmering, add the steak and cook until browned, about 2 minutes per side. Transfer the steak to a plate and set aside.

Add the chopped onion to the skillet you used for the steak, and cook over medium heat until soft and translucent, about 2 minutes. Add the sliced mushrooms and minced garlic, and cook until the mushrooms are browned, 5 minutes more. Sprinkle the flour over the mushroom mixture and cook, stirring, until it is incorporated, about 1 minute. Add the beef broth, red wine, salt, and pepper and continue to cook over medium heat until the sauce thickens, 2 minutes. Add the steak cubes and simmer gently over medium-low heat for 4 minutes. Then remove from the heat.

When adding yogurt or any dairy ingredient to a hot dish, tempering helps prevent curdling. To temper, place the yogurt in a small bowl and add a few tablespoons of the warmed sauce, soup, or whatever you are working with. Then the warmed dairy mixture can be gently stirred into the hot sauce.

Place the yogurt in a small bowl. Stir ¼ cup of the sauce into the yogurt. Then add the warm yogurt mixture to the skillet and stir to incorporate. Serve immediately.

SERVING SIZE: 1¼ cups

NUTRITION INFORMATION (PER SERVING): Calories: 360; Total Fat: 18 grams; Saturated Fat: 5 grams; Protein: 37 grams; Total Carbohydrates: 11 grams; Sugars: 4 grams; Fiber: 1 gram; Cholesterol: 94 milligrams; Sodium: 350 milligrams

Stuffed Peppers

When I was a little girl, one of my favorite dishes was my grandma's stuffed peppers. Over the years I have experimented with her original recipe and have created numerous mouth-watering versions using healthy add-ins. In this one, I kept the original beef and rice my grandma used, but added mozzarella cheese and dried apricots for a special twist.

Prep time: 15 minutes *Cook time:* 1 hour 50 minutes SERVES 4

½ cup white basmati rice
1 medium yellow onion
2 cloves garlic
1 tablespoon olive oil
8 ounces lean ground beef (90% or higher)
½ cup canned no-salt-added tomato sauce
2 dried basil leaves, crumbled (or 2 teaspoons crumbled dried basil)
¼ teaspoon salt
⅛ teaspoon freshly ground black pepper
Cooking spray
4 ounces part-skim mozzarella cheese
6 dried apricots
4 large red bell peppers
½ cup nonfat plain Greek yogurt
¼ cup chopped fresh chives

Combine ¾ cup water and the rice in a medium saucepan, and bring to a boil over high heat. Reduce the heat to low, cover the pan, and simmer until the rice is tender and most of the liquid has been absorbed, about 12 minutes. Remove from the heat and allow to stand, covered, for 5 minutes; then fluff the rice with a fork and set it aside.

Chop the onion. Mince the garlic. Heat the olive oil in a medium skillet over medium heat. When the oil is shimmering, add the chopped onion and sauté until soft and translucent, about 4 minutes. Add the minced garlic and continue to cook until fragrant, 30 seconds. Add the ground beef and cook, breaking it up with a spoon, until it is well browned, about 5 minutes. Add the tomato sauce, dried basil leaves, salt, and pepper and continue to cook until fragrant, 5 minutes. Then remove from the heat and set aside to cool for about 10 minutes.

Preheat the oven to 400°F. Coat a large baking dish with cooking spray and set it aside.

Cut the mozzarella into ¼-inch cubes. Chop the dried apricots. Place both in a large bowl, add the cooled beef mixture, and toss to combine.

Slice the tops off the bell peppers. Using a paring knife, gently remove the membrane and seeds. Spoon ¾ cup of the beef mixture into each cored bell pepper, and arrange the peppers in the prepared baking dish, leaving about 2 inches between them. Cover the dish with aluminum foil, and bake for 50 minutes. Then uncover and bake for another 20 minutes.

Meanwhile, stir the yogurt and chopped chives together in a small bowl.

Place a stuffed pepper on each of four plates. Spoon 2 tablespoons of the yogurt mixture over each one, and serve.

SERVING SIZE: 1 stuffed pepper and 2 tablespoons yogurt

NUTRITION INFORMATION (PER SERVING): Calories: 413; Total Fat: 16 grams; Saturated Fat: 6 grams; Protein: 26 grams; Total Carbohydrates: 42 grams; Sugars: 15 grams; Fiber: 6 grams; Cholesterol: 52 milligrams; Sodium: 425 milligrams

Penne Bolognese

I have a weakness for Bolognese sauce, but I often stay away from it in restaurants because of the ridiculously high calories in the sauce and the oversize pasta portions. When I do end up ordering it, my husband and I share the dish or I pack half to take home. In this lightened version, the creamy texture in the Bolognese sauce comes from the Greek yogurt, and the pasta portions are kept under control. The end result is a delicious and healthy meal for around 500 calories.

Prep time: 12 minutes *Cook time:* 30 minutes SERVES 6

- 4 teaspoons olive oil
- 1 medium yellow onion, chopped
- 4 cloves garlic, minced
- 1 pound lean ground beef sirloin
- 1 teaspoon granulated sugar
- 1 (28-ounce) can crushed tomatoes
- 3½ ounces (3 tablespoons) tomato paste
- 1 pound penne pasta, preferably whole-grain (I like Barilla or Ronzoni)
- 1 medium tomato, cut into ¼-inch dice
- 1 teaspoon garlic powder
- ⅛ teaspoon salt
- ⅛ teaspoon freshly ground black pepper
- 2 tablespoons low-fat plain Greek yogurt
- 3 tablespoons chopped fresh basil leaves

Fill a large pot with water and bring it to a boil over high heat.

While the water is heating, start the Bolognese sauce: In a large saucepan, heat 3 teaspoons of the olive oil over medium heat. When the oil is shimmering, add the chopped onion and minced garlic and sauté until the onion is soft and translucent, about 4 minutes. Add the ground beef, breaking it up with a spoon. Sprinkle with the sugar and stir to incorporate. Cook until the meat is well browned, about 5 minutes. Add the crushed tomatoes and tomato paste. Stir to combine thoroughly. Raise the heat to high and bring to a boil. Then reduce the heat to low and simmer for 10 minutes.

Add the penne to the boiling water and cook until al dente, 9 minutes. Drain the pasta and set it aside (do not rinse).

Finish the sauce: Stir in the diced tomato, garlic powder, salt, and pepper. Remove the saucepan from the heat and allow it to cool slightly.

In a small bowl, whisk together the remaining 1 teaspoon olive oil and the yogurt. Add the yogurt to the sauce and stir gently until incorporated.

To serve, spoon 1⅓ cups of the pasta onto each of six plates, and top with 1 cup of the meat sauce. Sprinkle ½ tablespoon of the chopped basil on top of each plate.

SERVING SIZE: 1⅓ cups pasta and 1 cup meat sauce

NUTRITION INFORMATION (PER SERVING): Calories: 514; Total Fat: 12 gram; Saturated Fat: 4 grams; Protein: 28 grams; Total Carbohydrates: 74 grams; Sugars: 6 grams; Fiber: 5 grams; Cholesterol: 49 milligrams; Sodium: 307 milligrams

Spaghetti Carbonara with Peas

This lightened version of an old favorite incorporates Canadian bacon and Parmesan cheese to boost the flavor. Many folks shy away from using these high-fat ingredients, but you don't have to! A small amount can enhance a dish while still keeping the calories within a reasonable limit. Everything in moderation!

Prep time: 20 minutes *Cook time:* 20 minutes SERVES 4

- Cooking spray
- 4 slices (1½ ounces) Canadian bacon
- 12 ounces whole-grain spaghetti
- 2 cups frozen peas
- 1 clove garlic
- 2 large pasteurized eggs
- 1 cup (3 ounces) grated Parmesan cheese
- ½ teaspoon salt
- ¼ teaspoon freshly ground black pepper
- 6 tablespoons nonfat plain Greek yogurt
- 1 tablespoon olive oil

Coat a large skillet with cooking spray and heat it over medium heat. When the spray is shimmering, add the bacon and cook until browned and crisp, about 6 minutes. Remove the bacon from the skillet. Dice the bacon and set it aside. Reserve the skillet.

In a large pot, bring 2 quarts water to a boil over high heat. Add the spaghetti and cook, stirring often. While the spaghetti is cooking, set a large colander in the sink and put the frozen peas in it. When the spaghetti is al dente (after about 9 minutes), reserve ¼ cup of the cooking water, and then drain the spaghetti over the peas to defrost them.

Grate the garlic. In a medium bowl, whisk together the grated garlic, eggs, cheese, salt, and pepper. Then add the reserved pasta water and whisk to combine. Add the yogurt and whisk until smooth.

Heat the olive oil in the reserved skillet over low heat. When the oil is shimmering, add the hot pasta and toss to combine. Pour in the egg mixture and warm the spaghetti and sauce while tossing continuously until the sauce thickens, about 2 minutes. Then add

Pasteurized eggs are heat-treated to kill any harmful bacteria that may be present. When cooking dishes where raw eggs may not get fully cooked, using pasteurized eggs ensures the eaters' safety.

the bacon and toss gently to combine. Divide the pasta among four plates and serve immediately.

SERVING SIZE: 1½ cups

NUTRITION INFORMATION (PER SERVING): Calories: 537; Total Fat: 15 grams; Saturated Fat: 5 grams; Protein: 35 grams; Total Carbohydrates: 68 grams; Sugars: 9 grams; Fiber: 9 grams; Cholesterol: 114 milligrams; Sodium: 977 milligrams

Spinach Macaroni Bake

When I was a senior in college, I shared a house with five fabulous women. It was the same year I began taking nutrition classes and started experimenting with healthy cooking techniques. Once I started cooking and eating healthier, the ten pounds I had gained as a freshman were quickly shed. This macaroni bake was a signature dish I often made for my roommates—they were always thankful for a home-cooked meal, especially during midterms and finals!

Prep time: 10 minutes *Cook time:* 50 minutes SERVES 6

- Cooking spray
- 8 ounces elbow macaroni pasta, preferably whole-grain (I like Barilla or Ronzoni)
- 10 ounces frozen chopped spinach, thawed and well drained
- 1 clove garlic, minced
- 1 (8-ounce) container part-skim ricotta
- ¼ cup nonfat plain Greek yogurt
- 1 teaspoon dried parsley flakes
- ¼ teaspoon dried basil
- 1 large egg, beaten
- ⅛ teaspoon crushed red pepper flakes
- ⅛ teaspoon salt
- ⅛ teaspoon freshly ground black pepper
- 2 cups jarred marinara sauce
- 1 cup shredded part-skim mozzarella cheese
- ¼ cup (¾ ounce) freshly grated Parmesan cheese

Preheat the oven to 350°F. Coat an 8 x 8-inch baking dish with cooking spray and set it aside.

Bring 4 quarts water to a boil in a large pot over high heat, add the pasta, and cook, stirring occasionally, until al dente, about 7 minutes. Drain the pasta completely and set it aside (do not rinse).

Pour 1 cup water into a medium saucepan, add the spinach, and bring to a boil over high heat. Cover, lower the heat to medium-low, and cook, stirring occasionally, until tender, 5 minutes. Drain the spinach, and set it aside to cool slightly, about 5 minutes.

In a large bowl, stir together the minced garlic, ricotta, yogurt, parsley flakes, basil, egg, red pepper flakes, salt, and black pepper. Add the pasta and the spinach, and toss to combine.

Spread 1 cup of the marinara sauce over the bottom of the prepared baking dish. Layer in half of the pasta mixture, then ½ cup each of the marinara sauce and the mozzarella. Repeat the layers of pasta, marinara, and mozzarella. Sprinkle the Parmesan cheese evenly over the top. Cover the baking dish loosely with aluminum foil, and bake until cooked through, 25 minutes. Then uncover and continue to bake until the cheese has browned, another 10 minutes.

Cut into 6 equal pieces, and serve warm.

SERVING SIZE: 1⅓ cups

NUTRITION INFORMATION (PER SERVING): Calories: 356; Total Fat: 11 grams; Saturated Fat: 5 grams; Protein: 20 grams; Total Carbohydrates: 45 grams; Sugars: 9 grams; Fiber: 5 grams; Cholesterol: 26 milligrams; Sodium: 705 milligrams

White Margherita Pizza

Part of the ricotta cheese in this version of the classic margherita pizza is replaced with Greek yogurt, cutting down on fat and cholesterol without diminishing the flavor. Topped with a combination of fresh and sun-dried tomatoes, plus delicious basil, it is a simple dish that will always satisfy.

Prep time: 15 minutes *Cook time:* 20 minutes

SERVES 4

- Cooking spray
- 3/4 cup part-skim ricotta cheese
- 1/4 cup nonfat plain Greek yogurt
- 1 medium plum tomato
- 4 ounces fresh mozzarella cheese
- 1 pound 100% whole wheat pizza dough, at room temperature
- Unbleached all-purpose flour, for dusting
- 1 tablespoon olive oil
- 8 sun-dried tomatoes
- 10 fresh basil leaves
- 1/8 teaspoon garlic powder

Preheat the oven to 425°F. Coat a pizza pan or baking sheet with cooking spray and set it aside.

In a small bowl, stir together the ricotta and yogurt. Set aside.

Cut the tomato into 1/8-inch-thick slices. Cut the mozzarella into 1/4-inch-thick slices. Roll out the pizza dough on a lightly floured surface to form a 12-inch round. Brush the entire surface with the olive oil. Spread the ricotta mixture over the dough, and then top with the sliced tomato, sliced mozzarella, sun-dried tomatoes, and basil leaves. Sprinkle with the garlic powder. Bake until the cheese is bubbling and the crust is crisp and browned around the edges, 20 minutes. Remove from the oven and allow to cool before cutting into 8 slices.

SERVING SIZE: 2 slices

NUTRITION INFORMATION (PER SERVING): Calories: 478; Total Fat: 17 grams; Saturated Fat: 6 grams; Protein: 22 grams; Total Carbohydrates: 57 grams; Sugars: 6 grams; Fiber: 9 grams; Cholesterol: 28 milligrams; Sodium: 895 milligrams

Quinoa Burgers

I first fell in love with quinoa burgers when I found premade ones at a local market. But then every time I was craving one, the store was sold out. To offset my disappointment, I took charge and created my own recipe—and haven't used store-bought since.

Prep time: 15 minutes *Cook time:* 55 minutes SERVES 4

- Cooking spray
- 2 cups low-sodium vegetable broth
- 1 cup quinoa
- 1 medium yellow onion
- 2 cloves garlic
- 3 ounces white mushrooms
- 1 tablespoon olive oil
- ¼ cup chopped fresh parsley
- ⅓ cup panko breadcrumbs
- 2 large eggs, beaten
- 2 tablespoons nonfat plain Greek yogurt
- ½ teaspoon salt
- ¼ teaspoon freshly ground black pepper

Preheat the oven to 375°F. Coat a baking sheet with cooking spray and set it aside.

Combine the vegetable broth and the quinoa in a medium saucepan and bring to a boil over high heat. Then reduce the heat to low, cover the pan, and simmer until the liquid has been absorbed, about 15 minutes. Remove from the heat, uncover, and set aside to cool.

Meanwhile, chop the onion. Mince the garlic. Chop the white mushrooms. Heat the olive oil in a large skillet over medium heat. When the oil is shimmering, add the chopped onion and sauté until soft and translucent, about 5 minutes. Add the minced garlic and cook until fragrant, 30 seconds. Then add the chopped mushrooms and cook until soft and browned, about 5 minutes. Remove the pan from the heat and set aside to cool.

In a large bowl, combine the cooked quinoa, onion-mushroom mixture, chopped parsley, panko breadcrumbs, eggs, yogurt, salt, and pepper. Stir to incorporate the ingredients. Scoop out ½ cup of the quinoa mixture and using clean hands, form it into a patty. Place the patty on the prepared baking sheet, and press down with the palm of your hand to flatten it slightly. Repeat with the remaining quinoa mixture, creating 8 patties total and leaving

2 inches between patties. Bake until lightly browned and warmed through, 25 to 30 minutes. Allow to cool for 10 minutes before serving.

SERVING SIZE: 2 burgers

NUTRITION INFORMATION (PER SERVING): Calories: 251; Total Fat: 8 grams; Saturated Fat: 1 gram; Protein: 11 grams; Total Carbohydrates: 36 grams; Sugars: 5 grams; Fiber: 4 grams; Cholesterol: 93 milligrams; Sodium: 424 milligrams

Spicy Indian-Style Lentils and Rice

My mom and I love Indian food. I don't get a chance to eat it often since my husband isn't a fan. When he's away, I'll invite my mom over and we'll spend some quality mother-daughter bonding time over this spicy dish.

Prep time: 10 minutes *Cook time:* 40 minutes SERVES 2

1 cup brown basmati rice
1 medium yellow onion
2 cloves garlic
3 medium carrots
1 portobello mushroom cap
1 (15-ounce) can brown lentils
2 teaspoons olive oil
½ teaspoon ground cumin
¼ teaspoon ground cinnamon
¼ teaspoon cayenne pepper
¼ teaspoon ground cardamom
¼ teaspoon freshly ground black pepper
1 cup low-sodium vegetable broth
¼ teaspoon kosher salt
2 tablespoons pine nuts
¼ cup chopped fresh cilantro
½ cup nonfat plain Greek yogurt
½ lemon, cut into 4 wedges

Bring 2 cups water to a boil in a medium saucepan over high heat. Add the basmati rice and return to a boil. Then lower the heat, cover the pan, and simmer until the rice is tender and the water has been absorbed, about 40 minutes. Fluff the rice with a fork and set aside.

While the rice is cooking, chop the onion. Mince the garlic. Peel the carrots and cut them into ½-inch-thick rounds. Cut the mushroom cap into ½-inch dice. Drain and rinse the lentils.

In a medium skillet, heat the olive oil over medium heat. When the oil is shimmering, add the chopped onion and cook until translucent, about 2 minutes. Add the garlic and cook until fragrant, 30 seconds. Add the carrots and cook until softened, 5 to 6 minutes. Add the mushrooms and cook until their liquid has been released and evaporated, 2 minutes. Add the drained lentils, cumin, cinnamon, cayenne, cardamom, and black pepper, and stir to incorporate. Add the vegetable broth and bring the mixture to a boil over high heat. Lower the heat and simmer until the flavors are incorporated, about 10 minutes. Remove the pan from the heat and stir in the salt. Set aside.

In a small sauté pan over medium-low heat, toast the pine nuts until fragrant and lightly browned, 3 to 4 minutes. Remove the pan from the heat and allow to cool for about 5 minutes.

Chop the cilantro. In a small bowl, stir together the chopped cilantro and the yogurt. To serve, spoon 1 cup basmati rice into each of two bowls. Spoon 1 cup of the lentil mixture over the rice. Top each bowl with ¼ cup of the yogurt-cilantro mixture and 1 tablespoon of the toasted pine nuts. Garnish with 2 lemon wedges.

SERVING SIZE: 1 bowl

NUTRITION INFORMATION (PER SERVING): Calories: 540; Total Fat: 14 grams; Saturated Fat: 1 gram; Protein: 18 grams; Total Carbohydrates: 92 grams; Sugars: 14 grams; Fiber: 10 grams; Cholesterol: 0 milligrams; Sodium: 458 milligrams

Artichoke, Fennel, and Ricotta-Stuffed Shells

The vegetables in these stuffed shells give this dish a unique flavor boost, while the tofu and Greek yogurt replace part of the ricotta, decreasing the saturated fat and cholesterol. It is a perfect dish to cook and freeze for later.

Prep time: 15 minutes *Cook time:* 35 minutes

SERVES 6

- 24 jumbo pasta shells
- ½ fennel bulb
- 2 teaspoons olive oil
- ¼ teaspoon salt
- ¼ teaspoon freshly ground black pepper
- 2 cups jarred marinara sauce
- ¼ cup dry white wine
- 4 ounces silken tofu
- 1 (9-ounce) package frozen artichoke hearts, thawed
- 1 sprig fresh thyme
- ¼ cup nonfat plain Greek yogurt
- 4 ounces (about ⅓ cup) part-skim ricotta cheese
- ¼ cup (¾ ounce) freshly grated Parmesan cheese
- ¼ cup chopped fresh basil

Preheat the oven to 425°F.

Bring 4 quarts water to a boil in a large pot over high heat. Add the shells and cook until al dente, about 10 minutes. Drain the pasta completely (do not rinse) and set aside to cool slightly.

Chop the fennel, white parts only. In a medium skillet, heat the olive oil over medium heat. When the oil is shimmering, add the chopped fennel and sauté until soft, about 5 minutes. Add ⅛ teaspoon each of the salt and pepper, and toss to combine. Remove the pan from the heat and set aside to cool.

In a small bowl, stir together 1 cup of the marinara sauce and the white wine. Pour this mixture evenly over the bottom of a 9 x 11-inch baking dish.

Drain and rinse the tofu and cut it into ¼-inch cubes. Drain the artichoke hearts and coarsely chop. Remove the thyme leaves from the stem. Place the fennel, cubed tofu, chopped artichokes, thyme leaves, yogurt, ricotta, and the remaining ⅛ teaspoon salt and pepper in a large bowl and toss to combine. Spoon 2 tablespoons of the artichoke mixture into each pasta shell. Arrange the stuffed shells in a single layer, leaving 1 inch between them, in the prepared baking dish. Top with the remaining 1 cup marinara sauce and sprinkle with the Parmesan cheese. Bake, uncovered, until lightly browned and cooked through, 20 minutes. Remove from the oven and allow to cool for 10 minutes. Sprinkle fresh basil on top before serving.

SERVING SIZE: 4 stuffed shells

NUTRITION INFORMATION (PER SERVING): Calories: 314; Total Fat: 8 grams; Saturated Fat: 2 grams; Protein: 13 grams; Total Carbohydrates: 49 grams; Sugars: 10 grams; Fiber: 6 grams; Cholesterol: 10 milligrams; Sodium: 571 milligrams

Stuffed Acorn Squash with Wild Rice and Pinto Beans

Every Thanksgiving my mom serves stuffed acorn squash. She makes all types of fillings, but one common ingredient is dried cranberries—which you will also find in my version.

Prep time: 15 minutes *Cook time:* 1 hour 10 minutes SERVES 4

- 1½ cups low-sodium vegetable broth
- ½ cup wild rice
- Cooking spray
- 4 acorn squash
- 2 tablespoons olive oil
- ¾ teaspoon salt
- ½ teaspoon freshly ground black pepper
- ½ cup frozen corn, thawed
- 2 shallots, chopped
- 2 cloves garlic, minced
- 1 (15-ounce) can no-salt-added pinto beans (I like Eden Foods)
- 1 large egg, beaten
- ¼ cup nonfat plain Greek yogurt
- ½ cup chopped fresh parsley
- ¼ cup chopped raw walnuts
- ⅓ cup dried cranberries

In a medium saucepan, bring the vegetable broth to a boil over high heat. Add the wild rice and return to a boil. Then lower the heat, cover the pan, and simmer until the rice is tender and the water has been absorbed, 40 to 50 minutes. Fluff the rice with a fork and set it aside to cool for about 10 minutes. Then spoon the rice into a large bowl.

While the rice is cooking, preheat the oven to 425°F. Coat a baking dish with cooking spray and set it aside.

Use a large knife to slice the tops off the acorn squash. Halve the squash lengthwise, and remove and discard the seeds. Brush the halves with 1 tablespoon of the olive oil and season with ¼ teaspoon each of the salt and pepper. Place the squash, cut side down, in the prepared baking dish and bake until tender, 25 to 30 minutes. Remove the baking dish from the oven and set aside to cool. When cool enough to handle, turn the squash right-side-up. Lower the oven temperature to 350°F.

Bring ½ cup water to a boil in a saucepan over high heat. When the water is boiling, add the corn and warm through for 2 to 3 minutes. Drain the corn and set it aside to cool for about 10 minutes.

Heat the remaining 1 tablespoon olive oil in a large skillet over medium heat. When the oil is shimmering, add the chopped shallots and cook until translucent, about 2 minutes. Add the garlic and cook until fragrant, 30 seconds. Mix in the pinto beans and cook, stirring occasionally, until warmed through, about 1 minute. Remove the skillet from the heat and set it aside to cool for about 10 minutes.

Add the corn and the bean mixture to the rice in the large bowl, and stir to combine. Then add the egg, yogurt, and remaining ½ teaspoon salt and ¼ teaspoon pepper; stir until incorporated. Fold in the chopped parsley, chopped walnuts, and dried cranberries until well incorporated.

Spoon a heaping ⅓ cup of the rice and bean mixture into each of the cooked acorn squash halves, still in the baking dish, and bake until the tops are browned, 15 to 20 minutes.

Remove the squash from the oven and place 2 acorn squash halves on each of four plates. Serve warm.

SERVING SIZE: 2 stuffed squash halves

NUTRITION INFORMATION (PER SERVING): Calories: 531; Total Fat: 15 grams; Saturated Fat: 2 grams; Protein: 18 grams; Total Carbohydrates: 90 grams; Sugars: 10 grams; Fiber: 15 grams; Cholesterol: 47 milligrams; Sodium: 549 milligrams

White Cheese and Broccoli Rabe Pizza

Pizza is one of the easiest dishes to throw together for a quick weeknight meal. I typically open my refrigerator and use whatever extra vegetables I find in there. I always feel good about adding veggies to my day, and it is a perfect way to keep food from going to waste! This recipe calls for broccoli rabe, but use whatever you have on hand.

Prep time: 10 minutes *Cook time:* 23 minutes SERVES 4

- Cooking spray
- 4 ounces broccoli rabe
- ⅛ teaspoon salt
- ⅛ teaspoon freshly ground black pepper
- ½ cup part-skim ricotta cheese
- 2 ounces soft goat cheese
- ¼ cup nonfat plain Greek yogurt
- 1 (10-ounce) ready-made whole wheat thin-crust pizza crust (I like Rustic Crust)
- 1 tablespoon canola oil
- 2 cloves garlic, thinly sliced

Preheat the oven to 375°F. Coat a pizza pan or baking sheet with cooking spray and set it aside.

Trim and coarsely chop the broccoli rabe. Fill a medium pot with 1 cup water, fit it with a steamer basket, and bring to a boil over high heat. Add the broccoli rabe, cover, and steam until tender, about 8 minutes. Remove the pot from the heat, remove the steamer basket, and set the broccoli rabe aside to cool. Place the cooled broccoli rabe in a medium bowl and season with the salt and pepper.

In a medium bowl, stir together the ricotta, goat cheese, and yogurt until well combined. Set aside.

Place the pizza crust on the prepared pan or baking sheet, and brush with the canola oil. Using a spatula, spread the ricotta mixture evenly over the crust. Then top evenly with the broccoli rabe and the garlic. Bake until the crust is crisp and browned around the edges, about 15 minutes. Remove from the oven and allow to cool slightly before cutting into 8 slices.

SERVING SIZE: 2 slices

NUTRITION INFORMATION (PER SERVING): Calories: 284; Total Fat: 10 grams; Saturated Fat: 4 grams; Protein: 14 grams; Total Carbohydrates: 39 grams; Sugars: 1 gram; Fiber: 7 grams; Cholesterol: 16 milligrams; Sodium: 408 milligrams

Mac and Cheese

This childhood favorite can rack up more than 1,000 calories per serving, not to mention all the unhealthy fat from the butter, milk, and cheese. Boxed versions are no healthier, made with faux cheese and brimming with sodium and preservatives. Here we lighten it up and portion it properly, ensuring maximum flavor for a reasonable number of calories.

Prep time: 15 minutes *Cook time:* 35 minutes SERVES 4

- 8 ounces fusilli pasta, preferably whole-grain (I like Barilla or Ronzoni)
- 2 tablespoons unsalted butter
- 1 tablespoon unbleached all-purpose flour
- 1½ cups reduced-fat milk
- ¼ teaspoon smoked paprika
- 1 large egg
- ½ cup low-fat plain Greek yogurt
- ⅛ teaspoon kosher salt
- 6 ounces low-fat sharp cheddar cheese, shredded (1½ cups)
- ½ cup panko breadcrumbs

Preheat the oven to 350°F.

Bring 4 quarts water to a boil in a large pot over high heat. Add the fusilli pasta and cook until al dente, 8 to 10 minutes. Drain the pasta completely (do not rinse) and place in a large mixing bowl. Set aside.

Place 1 tablespoon of the butter and the flour in a medium saucepan, and warm over medium-low heat, stirring continuously to avoid lumps, until thickened, about 1 minute. Add the milk and paprika, stirring to combine thoroughly. Raise the heat to medium and bring the mixture to a slow boil, stirring every 30 seconds. Then reduce the heat to low and simmer for about 10 minutes, stirring every 45 to 60 seconds to maintain a smooth consistency.

Crack the egg into a small bowl and beat the egg. Slowly add 1 tablespoon of the sauce to the egg, mixing continuously to avoid scrambling the egg. Repeat with 4 or 5 more table-spoons of the sauce to bring up the temperature of the egg; then stir the warm mixture back into the sauce.

Stir the yogurt and salt into the sauce. Reserving ¼ cup of the cheddar cheese, gradually add the rest to the sauce, stirring it in to maintain a smooth texture. When the cheese is completely melted and incorporated, remove the pan from the heat and add the sauce to the pasta. Fold together, and transfer to a 9 x 9-inch baking dish.

To make the topping, melt the remaining 1 tablespoon butter in a small saucepan over low heat. Add the panko breadcrumbs and toss to coat, toasting the breadcrumbs until lightly browned. Remove the pan from the heat. Sprinkle the reserved ¼ cup cheddar cheese over the pasta in the baking dish, and then top with the breadcrumbs.

Bake until bubbling and golden brown, about 15 minutes. Remove from the oven and allow to cool for at least 10 minutes before serving.

SERVING SIZE: 1¼ cups

NUTRITION INFORMATION (PER SERVING): Calories: 507; Total Fat: 19 grams; Saturated Fat: 12 grams; Protein: 27 grams; Total Carbohydrates: 55 grams; Sugars: 2 grams; Fiber: 2 grams; Cholesterol: 100 milligrams; Sodium: 524 milligrams

Spaghetti Squash Alfredo

I love any teachable moment when it comes to food. Every time I slice open a spaghetti squash, my kids gather around to watch its strands miraculously turn into "spaghetti." Once the meal is served, they are still chatting about how cool this veggie is!

Prep time: 40 minutes *Cook time:* 1 hour SERVES 2

- 1 medium spaghetti squash
- 1 tablespoon olive oil
- 2 cloves garlic, minced
- 1 carrot, peeled and grated
- ¾ cup nonfat evaporated milk
- ½ cup nonfat plain Greek yogurt
- ¾ cup baby arugula, chopped
- 6 cherry tomatoes, quartered
- ¼ cup freshly grated Parmesan cheese, plus 2 tablespoons for sprinkling (1 ounce total)
- ¼ teaspoon salt
- ¼ teaspoon freshly ground black pepper

Wash the spaghetti squash to remove any visible dirt. Place the squash in a large stockpot and add enough water to cover it. Bring the water to a boil over high heat, and cook for 30 minutes. Using tongs, carefully remove the squash from the hot water. Slice it in half lengthwise, and return the halves to the boiling water. Cook until tender, about 20 minutes. Drain, and set aside to cool for about 15 minutes. Scoop out the seeds from the spaghetti squash, using a spoon. With a fork, scrape the flesh out to create spaghetti-like strands; set aside. Do not discard the shell of the two squash halves.

Preheat the broiler.

In a medium saucepan, heat the olive oil over medium heat. Add the minced garlic and grated carrot, and cook until softened, about 1 minute. Add the evaporated milk and bring to a boil over high heat. Then reduce the heat to low and simmer until incorporated, 1 minute. Remove from the heat and allow the mixture to cool for 2 minutes. Then stir in the yogurt until combined. Add the spaghetti squash, chopped arugula, quartered tomatoes, ¼ cup Parmesan cheese, salt, and pepper and stir until warmed through, about 1 minute.

Divide the mixture evenly between each of the hollowed-out squash halves and sprinkle with the remaining 2 tablespoons Parmesan cheese. Place the squash halves on a baking sheet and cook under the broiler until the cheese is bubbly, about 2 minutes. Remove the baking sheet from the broiler and allow to cool slightly, about 5 minutes.

Place 1 filled squash half on each of two plates. Serve warm.

SERVING SIZE: 1 squash half with 2 cups filling

NUTRITION INFORMATION (PER SERVING): Calories: 445; Total Fat: 15 grams; Saturated Fat: 4 grams; Protein: 24 grams; Total Carbohydrates: 63 grams; Sugars: 17 grams; Fiber: 2 grams; Cholesterol: 13 milligrams; Sodium: 791 milligrams

Naan Bread Pizza with Olives, Mushrooms, and Peppers

Whole wheat naan bread, with its soft and chewy texture, has become a favorite in my home. As a fun activity, I have each of my daughters create her own pizza using her favorite toppings—and olives are at the top of both their lists!

Prep time: 10 minutes *Cook time:* 12 minutes

SERVES 4

- Cooking spray
- 2 (4.5-ounce) whole-grain naan breads (I like Stonefire)
- 1 tablespoon grapeseed oil
- ½ cup part-skim ricotta cheese
- ¼ cup nonfat plain Greek yogurt
- 3 ounces (about 3 medium) white mushrooms, sliced
- ½ medium red bell pepper, cut into ½-inch strips
- ¼ cup pitted canned black olives, halved

Preheat the oven to 375°F. Coat a pizza pan or baking sheet with cooking spray and set it aside.

Brush the naan breads with the grapeseed oil. In a small bowl, combine the ricotta and yogurt. Spread the ricotta mixture evenly over the two naan breads. Top each bread with half of the mushrooms, bell peppers, and black olives. Place on the prepared pan or baking sheet and bake until the crust is crisp and browned around the edges, 12 to 15 minutes. Remove from the oven and allow to cool slightly before slicing each pizza in half.

SERVING SIZE: 1 piece

NUTRITION INFORMATION (PER SERVING): Calories: 282; Total Fat: 12 grams; Saturated Fat: 3 grams; Protein: 11 grams; Total Carbohydrates: 32 grams; Sugars: 5 grams; Fiber: 5 grams; Cholesterol: 15 milligrams; Sodium: 500 milligrams

Grapeseed oil has a light, nutty flavor and can be heated to high temperatures. It's easy to find in almost any market. I sometimes like to use it in place of canola oil because it's high in polyunsaturated fats and antioxidants.

CHAPTER 6

Side Dishes

Baked Sweet Potato with Cinnamon and Pecans

Growing up as a picky eater, I only began to enjoy sweet potatoes as a young adult—but now I eat them every chance I get. This version is topped with a combination of tastiness to help bring out the potato's natural sweetness.

Prep time: 15 minutes *Cook time:* 54 minutes

SERVES 4

- 1 ounce (¼ cup) raw pecans
- 4 medium sweet potatoes
- ½ cup nonfat vanilla Greek yogurt
- ½ teaspoon ground cinnamon
- ⅛ teaspoon ground nutmeg
- ¼ teaspoon salt
- ¼ teaspoon freshly ground black pepper

Preheat the oven to 400°F.

Chop the pecans, place them in a medium skillet, and toast over medium heat until browned and fragrant, about 4 minutes. Remove the pan from the heat and set aside.

Pierce each potato several times with a fork. Place on a baking sheet and bake until tender, about 50 minutes. Remove from the oven and carefully make a lengthwise slit at the top of each potato. Pry the slit open with a fork. Allow to cool for 10 minutes.

In a small bowl, stir together the yogurt, cinnamon, and nutmeg. Sprinkle the potatoes evenly with the salt and pepper, and then top each one with 2 tablespoons of the yogurt mixture and 1 tablespoon of the pecans.

SERVING SIZE: 1 potato with toppings

NUTRITION INFORMATION (PER SERVING): Calories: 183; Total Fat: 5 grams; Saturated Fat: 0 grams; Protein: 6 grams; Total Carbohydrates: 30 grams; Sugars: 8 grams; Fiber: 5 grams; Cholesterol: 0 milligrams; Sodium: 230 milligrams

Choose sweet potatoes that are firm to the touch and that do not have large dents or blemishes on the skin. You can store them in a cool, dry place for up to 4 weeks. Cooked sweet potatoes can also be stored in the refrigerator for 5 to 7 days, or the freezer for 6 to 9 months.

Silken Mashed Potatoes

Not a fan of lumpy mashed potatoes? Yukon Golds are the perfect choice for silky-smooth spuds. To lighten the dish, a combination of low-fat milk, Greek yogurt, and just a dab of butter adds flavor with far less fat than in traditional mashed potatoes.

Prep time: 20 minutes *Cook time:* 12 minutes

SERVES 8

- 3 pounds Yukon Gold potatoes
- 3 cloves garlic
- ½ cup low-fat plain Greek yogurt
- ½ cup low-fat milk
- 1 tablespoon unsalted butter, at room temperature
- ¾ teaspoon salt
- ¼ teaspoon freshly ground black pepper
- 3 scallions, chopped (white and green parts)

Wash, peel, and quarter the potatoes. Place them in a large pot, cover with cold water, and bring to a boil over high heat. Cook until the potatoes are tender, about 12 minutes. Drain and set aside to cool slightly, about 5 minutes.

Mince the garlic. In a large bowl, whisk together the minced garlic, yogurt, milk, butter, salt, and pepper. Add the cooked potatoes and toss. Using an immersion blender, puree the potatoes until silky smooth, about 45 seconds, taking care not to overmix.

Place the mashed potatoes in a serving dish and garnish with the chopped scallions.

SERVING SIZE: ¾ cup

NUTRITION INFORMATION (PER SERVING): Calories: 169; Total Fat: 2 grams; Saturated Fat: 1 gram; Protein: 6 grams; Total Carbohydrates: 32 grams; Sugars: 1 gram; Fiber: 2 grams; Cholesterol: 5 milligrams; Sodium: 245 milligrams

The starch content of potatoes varies according to the type of potato. Yukon Golds have a medium starch content; they become moist when baked and are perfect for mashing, hash browns, or potato pancakes.

Quinoa with Roasted Butternut Squash

Although commonly referred to as a grain, quinoa is technically a seed. It is brimming with good-for-you nutrients like fiber, protein, thiamin, vitamin B_6, folate, zinc, potassium, selenium, and iron. Quinoa is one of the few plant foods that contain all the essential amino acids (the building blocks of protein), making it a unique and protein-packed food.

Prep time: 12 minutes *Cook time:* 57 minutes SERVES 6

- 1 small butternut squash
- 1 tablespoon olive oil
- 1 cup quinoa
- 2 tablespoons nonfat plain Greek yogurt
- 1 teaspoon apple cider vinegar
- ⅛ teaspoon salt
- ⅛ teaspoon freshly ground black pepper
- 2 tablespoons chopped fresh chives
- ½ cup slivered blanched almonds
- ¼ cup dried cranberries

Preheat the oven to 400°F.

Cut the butternut squash in half lengthwise. Using a spoon, scoop out the seeds, then cut each half again for a total of 4 quarters. Place the squash, cut side up, on a baking sheet and drizzle with the olive oil. Roast in the oven until softened, about 45 minutes. Remove the baking sheet from the oven and allow the squash to cool for 10 minutes. Remove the skin and dice the flesh into ½-inch cubes.

While the squash is roasting, combine the quinoa and 2 cups water in a medium saucepan and bring to a boil over high heat. Reduce the heat, cover the pan, and simmer until all the liquid has been absorbed, at least 12 minutes. Remove the pan from the heat and fluff the quinoa with a fork.

In a small bowl, stir together the yogurt, vinegar, salt, and pepper.

In a large bowl, toss together the squash, quinoa, chopped chives, almonds, and cranberries. Add the yogurt mixture and stir until incorporated.

SERVING SIZE: ¾ cup

NUTRITION INFORMATION (PER SERVING): Calories: 216; Total Fat: 8 grams; Saturated Fat: 1 gram; Protein: 6 grams; Total Carbohydrates: 33 grams; Sugars: 6 grams; Fiber: 5 grams; Cholesterol: 0 milligrams; Sodium: 62 milligrams

Mexican-Style Creamed Corn

This unique blend of corn, jalapeño, and Cotija cheese adds a Mexican flair to your everyday creamed corn—it just has less fat and fewer calories.

Prep time: 10 minutes *Cook time:* 15 minutes SERVES 6

- 2 cloves garlic
- 1 small yellow onion
- 1 jalapeño pepper
- 1 tablespoon olive oil
- 16 ounces frozen whole-kernel sweet corn
- ¼ teaspoon salt
- ⅛ teaspoon freshly ground black pepper
- 1 cup reduced-fat milk
- ⅓ cup low-fat plain Greek yogurt
- 2 ounces Cotija or ricotta salata cheese, crumbled (about ½ cup)

Mince the garlic. Chop the onion. Halve the jalapeño lengthwise, discard the seeds, and finely chop. In a medium saucepan, heat the olive oil over medium heat. Add the minced garlic and chopped onion, and sauté until the onion is soft and translucent, about 3 minutes. Add the chopped jalapeño, corn, salt, and pepper and stir to combine. Cook, stirring every 30 seconds, until the vegetables soften, 2 minutes. Add the milk and continue to stir. Raise the heat to high and bring to a boil; then reduce the heat to low and simmer for 10 minutes, stirring regularly. Remove the saucepan from the heat and set it aside.

Place the yogurt in a small bowl. Slowly stir 1 tablespoon of the corn mixture into the yogurt. Repeat, adding 1 tablespoon of the corn mixture three more times. Then stir the warmed yogurt into the corn mixture in the saucepan.

Pour the corn into a serving dish, top evenly with the crumbled cheese, and serve warm.

Cotija and ricotta salata are white, crumbly cheeses that can be found in the specialty cheese section at your market. They both have a salty flavor, perfect to scatter over salads, casseroles, tacos, chili, and of course creamed corn.

SERVING SIZE: ½ cup

NUTRITION INFORMATION (PER SERVING): Calories: 167; Total Fat: 6 grams; Saturated Fat: 2 grams; Protein: 7 grams; Total Carbohydrates: 22 grams; Sugars: 7 grams; Fiber: 2 grams; Cholesterol: 8 milligrams; Sodium: 109 milligrams

Roasted Asparagus with Hollandaise Sauce

Say good-bye to artery-clogging hollandaise sauce and hello to a deliciously healthy version! Even the most passionate hollandaise lover won't be able to tell the difference.

Prep time: 15 minutes *Cook time:* 20 minutes SERVES 4

- 1 clove garlic
- 1 pound asparagus spears
- 1 tablespoon olive oil
- ¼ teaspoon plus ⅛ teaspoon kosher salt
- ¼ teaspoon freshly ground black pepper
- ½ cup nonfat plain Greek yogurt
- 1 tablespoon unsalted butter, at room temperature
- 2 large egg yolks
- 1 teaspoon fresh lemon juice
- ½ teaspoon Dijon mustard
- ⅛ teaspoon cayenne pepper

Preheat the oven to 400°F.

Mince the garlic. Break off the tough ends of the asparagus spears. In a medium bowl, whisk together the minced garlic, olive oil, the ¼ teaspoon salt, and the black pepper. Add the asparagus and toss to coat. Arrange the asparagus in an even layer on a baking sheet and roast in the oven until tender and beginning to brown at the tips, 15 to 18 minutes.

Meanwhile, in a medium bowl, whisk together the yogurt, butter, egg yolks, lemon juice, mustard, cayenne, and remaining ⅛ teaspoon salt. Heat the mixture in the top of a double boiler set over simmering water (see the box on page 42), whisking continuously until it thickens, about 5 minutes. Immediately remove from the heat.

Place the asparagus in a serving dish and drizzle with the hollandaise sauce. Serve immediately.

SERVING SIZE: About 5 asparagus spears and 2 tablespoons sauce

NUTRITION INFORMATION (PER SERVING): Calories: 123; Total Fat: 9 grams; Saturated Fat: 3 grams; Protein: 7 grams; Total Carbohydrates: 6 grams; Sugars: 3 grams; Fiber: 2 grams; Cholesterol: 100 milligrams; Sodium: 204 milligrams

Asparagus contains a plant compound called asparagine, which contributes to its diuretic effect. It is also the reason some folks notice a strange odor in their urine after eating it.

Sautéed Chickpeas with Carrots and Parsley

Reminiscent of my summers in Israel, this combination makes a delicious side to fish or chicken. You can also toss it onto a bed of fresh spinach or stuff it into a whole wheat pita for a vegetarian main dish.

Prep time: 5 minutes *Cook time:* 5 minutes SERVES 4

- ½ medium yellow onion
- 2 medium carrots
- 2 teaspoons olive oil
- ¼ teaspoon ground turmeric
- 1 (15-ounce) can no-salt-added chickpeas, drained and rinsed
- 1 tablespoon honey
- ¼ teaspoon salt
- ⅛ teaspoon freshly ground black pepper
- ¼ cup chopped fresh parsley
- ½ cup nonfat plain Greek yogurt

Chop the onion. Peel and grate the carrots. In a medium saucepan, heat the olive oil over medium heat. Add the chopped onion and cook until softened and translucent, about 2 minutes. Add the turmeric and cook for 30 seconds, until fragrant. Add the grated carrots and cook until slightly softened, 1 minute. Add the chickpeas, honey, salt, and pepper and continue to cook until the flavors combine, 2 to 3 minutes.

In a small bowl, stir the chopped parsley and yogurt together until well incorporated.

To serve, spoon ½ cup of the chickpea mixture onto each of four plates and top with 2 tablespoons of the yogurt.

SERVING SIZE: ½ cup chickpeas and 2 tablespoons yogurt

NUTRITION INFORMATION (PER SERVING): Calories: 166; Total Fat: 3 grams; Saturated Fat: 0 grams; Protein: 9 grams; Total Carbohydrates: 26 grams; Sugars: 6 grams; Fiber: 5 grams; Cholesterol: 0 milligrams; Sodium: 190 milligrams

Kicked-Up Cheddar-Potato Casserole

The secret ingredient in this potato casserole is Sriracha. The American version of this Thai-inspired chili sauce was introduced in the early 1980s in Los Angeles, California. It is made from chile peppers, garlic, vinegar, sugar, and salt, and has a delicious balance of spicy, tangy, and sweet. Pick up a bottle at your local grocery or even at your local fish market. It is usually located in the Asian foods aisle.

Prep time: 20 minutes *Cook time:* 55 minutes SERVES 6

- 2 pounds red potatoes
- 1 small yellow onion
- 2 teaspoons olive oil
- Cooking spray
- ¾ cup reduced-fat milk
- ½ cup nonfat plain Greek yogurt
- 1 tablespoon Sriracha sauce
- 1 tablespoon unsalted butter
- 2 ounces reduced-fat sharp cheddar cheese, shredded (½ cup)

Wash and quarter the potatoes. Place them in a medium pot and add water to cover by 1 inch. Bring to a boil over high heat and cook until the potatoes are tender, about 18 minutes. Remove the pot from the heat, drain the potatoes, and set them aside to cool.

Meanwhile, dice the onion. Heat the olive oil in a small saucepan over medium heat. When the oil is shimmering, add the chopped onion and sauté until tender, about 3 minutes. Remove the pan from the heat and set it aside to cool slightly.

Preheat the oven to 350°F. Coat an 8 x 8-inch baking dish with cooking spray and set it aside.

Place the potatoes in a large bowl and add the milk. Using a potato masher or a fork, coarsely mash the potatoes. Fold in the sautéed onion. In a small bowl, whisk together the yogurt and Sriracha, and then fold this into the potato mixture. Place the potato mixture in the prepared baking dish.

Chop the butter into small cubes and scatter them evenly over the potato mixture. Place the baking dish in the oven and bake until the top begins to crisp, about 30 minutes. Then carefully remove the dish from the oven and turn on the broiler. Sprinkle the cheese evenly over the potatoes and broil until the cheese is melted and the top is golden brown, 1 to 2 minutes. Remove from the oven and allow to cool for 5 minutes before serving.

SERVING SIZE: ¾ cup

NUTRITION INFORMATION (PER SERVING): Calories: 203; Total Fat: 6 grams; Saturated Fat: 3 grams; Protein: 9 grams; Total Carbohydrates: 29 grams; Sugars: 6 grams; Fiber: 3 grams; Cholesterol: 14 milligrams; Sodium: 168 milligrams

Mashed Cauliflower au Gratin

The secret in this dish is roasting the cauliflower before mashing it. Doing so brings out the natural sweetness of this low-calorie vegetable that will have everyone begging for seconds.

Prep time: 20 minutes *Cook time:* 45 minutes SERVES 10

- Cooking spray
- 2½ pounds cauliflower florets
- 3 tablespoons olive oil
- ¼ teaspoon kosher salt
- ¼ teaspoon freshly ground black pepper
- 2 cloves garlic
- ¼ cup low-fat plain Greek yogurt
- ¼ cup low-fat milk
- 1 cup shredded reduced-fat Mexican cheese blend

Preheat the oven to 450°F. Coat an 8 x 8-inch baking dish with cooking spray and set it aside.

Coarsely chop the cauliflower florets and place them in a large bowl. Add the olive oil and ⅛ teaspoon each of the salt and pepper. Toss to evenly coat. Arrange the cauliflower in an even layer on a baking sheet, and roast in the oven until lightly browned, 30 to 35 minutes. Remove the baking sheet from the oven and set aside to cool for at least 10 minutes. Lower the oven temperature to 375°F.

Mince the garlic. In a large bowl, using a potato masher or a fork, mash the roasted cauliflower. Add the minced garlic, yogurt, milk, and the remaining ⅛ teaspoon salt and pepper. Mix to combine.

Place the cauliflower mixture in the prepared baking dish, and sprinkle the shredded cheese evenly over the top. Bake until the top is bubbling and lightly browned, about 15 minutes.

SERVING SIZE: ½ cup

NUTRITION INFORMATION (PER SERVING): Calories: 105; Total Fat: 7 grams; Saturated Fat: 2 grams; Protein: 6 grams; Total Carbohydrates: 6 grams; Sugars: 3 grams; Fiber: 2 grams; Cholesterol: 9 milligrams; Sodium: 177 milligrams

Part of the cruciferous vegetable (or cabbage) family, cauliflower contains numerous cancer-preventing antioxidants.

Cheddar-Jalapeño Bread

While living on the Upper East Side of Manhattan, I used to frequent a Mexican restaurant that served spicy jalapeño corn bread. Definitely a tasty idea, but corn bread tends to be hefty in calories. My quick version combines jalapeño, scallions, and 3/4 cup of sharp cheddar cheese. You don't need a lot of cheese—just a potent one to kick the flavor up a notch.

Prep time: 15 minutes *Cook time:* 40 minutes SERVES 10

- Cooking spray
- 1 scallion
- 1 jalapeño pepper
- 2¼ cups unbleached all-purpose flour
- 2 teaspoons baking powder
- ½ teaspoon baking soda
- 1 teaspoon salt
- 3 ounces extra-sharp cheddar cheese, shredded (¾ cup)
- ¾ cup nonfat plain Greek yogurt
- ½ cup low-fat milk
- 2 large eggs
- 2 tablespoons canola oil
- 3 tablespoons freshly grated Parmesan cheese

Preheat the oven to 400°F. Coat an 8-inch loaf pan with cooking spray and set it aside.

Chop the scallion, both white and green parts. Halve the jalapeño lengthwise, discard the seeds, and finely chop. In a large bowl, sift together the flour, baking powder, baking soda, and salt. Stir in the cheese, chopped scallion, and chopped jalapeño until thoroughly incorporated.

In a medium bowl, combine the yogurt, milk, eggs, and canola oil. Stir until the mixture is thick, with a buttermilk-like consistency.

Make a well in the center of the dry ingredients and pour in the wet ingredients. Stir with as few strokes as possible until just mixed. Pour into the prepared loaf pan and smooth the top with the back of a spoon. Sprinkle evenly with the Parmesan cheese. Bake on the center rack in the oven until a toothpick inserted into the center comes out clean, 40 minutes.

Be careful not to overmix the batter, or you will end up with a tough, dense bread.

SERVING SIZE: 1 (¾-inch) slice

NUTRITION INFORMATION (PER SERVING): Calories: 181; Total Fat: 6 grams; Saturated Fat: 2 grams; Protein: 9 grams; Total Carbohydrates: 22 grams; Sugars: 2 grams; Fiber: 1 gram; Cholesterol: 46 milligrams; Sodium: 555 milligrams

Cinnamon-Raisin Noodle Kugel

When I was a little girl, my mom always made a sweet raisin kugel for the holidays. She usually made the full-fat version, which was fantastic but laden with calories. To re-create my childhood experience with fewer calories, a combination of part-skim ricotta cheese, nonfat Greek yogurt, and low-fat evaporated milk creates a creamy texture, while crushed pineapple and golden raisins provide natural sweetness.

Prep time: 10 minutes *Cook time:* 38 minutes

SERVES 8

- 1 tablespoon canola oil
- 8 ounces wide curly egg noodles
- 1 (8-ounce) can crushed pineapple in its own juices or water, drained
- 8 ounces part-skim ricotta cheese
- ½ cup nonfat plain Greek yogurt
- ¾ cup low-fat evaporated milk
- ½ cup seedless golden raisins
- ⅓ cup packed light brown sugar
- 1 large egg, beaten
- 1 teaspoon vanilla extract
- 1 teaspoon ground cinnamon
- ¼ teaspoon salt

Preheat the oven to 375°F. Brush an 8 x 8-inch baking dish with the canola oil. Set aside.

Bring 4 quarts water to a boil in a large pot over high heat. Add the noodles and cook until al dente, about 8 minutes. Drain the noodles completely (do not rinse). Set aside to cool.

In a large bowl, combine the pineapple, ricotta, yogurt, evaporated milk, raisins, brown sugar, egg, vanilla extract, cinnamon, and salt; stir together well. Add the noodles and toss to coat evenly.

Place the noodle mixture in the prepared baking dish and distribute it evenly. Bake, uncovered, until the kugel is lightly browned, about 30 minutes. Remove baking dish from the oven and allow kugel to cool for 10 minutes before cutting into eight 2 x 4-inch squares.

SERVING SIZE: 1 (2 x 4-inch) square

NUTRITION INFORMATION (PER SERVING): Calories: 275; Total Fat: 6 grams; Saturated Fat: 2 grams; Protein: 11 grams; Total Carbohydrates: 44 grams; Sugars: 20 grams; Fiber: 2 grams; Cholesterol: 60 milligrams; Sodium: 161 milligrams

Coleslaw with Lemon, Chile, and Mint

This coleslaw has no mayo in sight! The combination of refreshing mint and spicy jalapeño will have your taste buds dancing. Serve it as a side with burgers, barbecued chicken, or turkey sandwiches.

Prep time: 20 minutes, plus 30 minutes refrigeration *Cook time:* 0 minutes SERVES 6

- ¼ cup fresh mint
- 1 jalapeño pepper
- 1 cup nonfat plain Greek yogurt
- 2 tablespoons olive oil
- Grated zest of 1 lemon
- ½ teaspoon light brown sugar
- 4 cups shredded green cabbage
- 1 cup shredded red cabbage
- 1 cup peeled and shredded carrot
- ½ teaspoon salt

Chop the mint leaves. Halve the jalapeño lengthwise, discard the seeds, and finely mince. In a large bowl, combine the chopped mint, minced jalapeño, yogurt, olive oil, lemon zest, and brown sugar. Stir until smooth. Set aside for at least 5 minutes to allow the flavors to combine.

Add the green and red cabbage, carrot, and salt, and toss evenly to coat. Cover, and chill in the refrigerator for at least 30 minutes before serving. The coleslaw will keep, covered, in the refrigerator for up to 3 days.

SERVING SIZE: 1 cup

NUTRITION INFORMATION (PER SERVING): Calories: 89; Total Fat: 5 grams; Saturated Fat: 1 gram; Protein: 5 grams; Total Carbohydrates: 8 grams; Sugars: 5 grams; Fiber: 3 grams; Cholesterol: 0 milligrams; Sodium: 379 milligrams

Edamame, Cherry Tomatoes, and Snap Peas

Baby soybeans, cherry tomatoes, snap peas, and red onions make this a colorful side dish. Tossed in a combination of balsamic vinegar, Greek yogurt, and spicy mustard, it has a simple, clean flavor that goes well with most every dish.

Prep time: 15 minutes *Cook time:* 0 minutes SERVES 8

- 1 cup frozen shelled edamame
- 1 pint cherry tomatoes
- 1 cup sugar snap peas
- ½ medium red onion
- 2 tablespoons balsamic vinegar
- 2 tablespoons nonfat plain Greek yogurt
- ½ teaspoon spicy brown mustard
- ⅛ teaspoon salt
- ⅛ teaspoon freshly ground black pepper
- 3 tablespoons grapeseed oil

Bring a small pot of water to a boil over high heat. Add the edamame and cook until heated through, about 5 minutes. Drain, and set aside to cool for at least 10 minutes.

Halve the cherry tomatoes. Cut the snap peas into thirds. Finely chop the red onion. In a medium bowl, combine the vegetables with the edamame; then set aside.

In a small bowl, whisk together the vinegar, yogurt, mustard, salt, and pepper. Slowly drizzle in the grapeseed oil, continuing to whisk until emulsified.

Pour the dressing over the edamame-tomato mixture, and toss to coat evenly.

SERVING SIZE: ½ cup

NUTRITION INFORMATION (PER SERVING): Calories: 86; Total Fat: 6 grams; Saturated Fat: 1 gram; Protein: 3 grams; Total Carbohydrates: 5 grams; Sugars: 3 grams; Fiber: 1 gram; Cholesterol: 0 milligrams; Sodium: 47 milligrams

Potato Salad with Parsnips and Edamame

Parsnips add a sweet nutty flavor to this potato salad, while the edamame bring protein and a gorgeous green hue. The Asian-inspired dressing perfectly flavors these delicious vegetables without drowning them in gobs of mayonnaise.

Prep time: 12 minutes *Cook time:* 15 minutes SERVES 6

- 1 pound medium-size red potatoes
- 8 ounces parsnips
- ½ cup frozen shelled edamame
- 2 medium scallions
- 3 tablespoons light mayonnaise
- 3 tablespoons nonfat plain Greek yogurt
- 1 tablespoon low-sodium soy sauce
- 1 tablespoon rice vinegar
- ½ teaspoon salt
- ¼ teaspoon freshly ground black pepper

Cut the potatoes into ½-inch cubes. Peel the parsnips and cut into ¼-inch-thick slices. Pour ½ cup water into a medium pot fitted with a steamer basket, and bring to a boil over high heat. Add the cubed potatoes and sliced parsnips, cover the pot, and lower the heat to medium. Cook until the vegetables are tender, 10 minutes. Remove from the pot and set aside to cool for at least 10 minutes.

Fill the same pot (without the basket) with water and bring to a boil over high heat. Add the edamame and lower the heat to medium. Cook for about 5 minutes, until heated through. Drain, and set aside to cool for 5 minutes. In a large bowl, combine the cooled potatoes, parsnips, and edamame.

Chop the scallions, both whites and greens. In a medium bowl, whisk together the chopped scallions, mayonnaise, yogurt, soy sauce, vinegar, salt, and pepper. Add this dressing to the potatoes mixture, and mix gently to combine.

Look for firm and smooth parsnips that are medium in size, avoiding those that are shriveled, spotted, or limp. You can store them in a plastic bag in the refrigerator for up to 4 weeks.

SERVING SIZE: 1 cup

NUTRITION INFORMATION (PER SERVING): Calories: 145; Total Fat: 3 grams; Saturated Fat: 1 gram; Protein: 5 grams; Total Carbohydrates: 25 grams; Sugars: 5 grams; Fiber: 4 grams; Cholesterol: 3 milligrams; Sodium: 358 milligrams

Zucchini Ribbons in Creamy Roasted Red Pepper Sauce

One of my favorite family activities is to go vegetable picking. We have been driving up to the same farm in Poughquag, New York, for the past seven years. I tend to schedule our trips towards the end of the summer so we can pick up summer goodies like peaches and zucchini. After I collect my bounty and bring it home, I always have extra. The extra zucchinis get whipped up into this quick, healthy side.

Prep time: 15 minutes *Cook time:* 1 minute

SERVES: 6

- 3 large (about 1½ pounds) zucchini
- 1 medium yellow or orange bell pepper
- 6 ounces jarred sweet roasted red peppers, drained
- ½ cup nonfat plain Greek yogurt

Holding the zucchini at the base, use a vegetable peeler to peel the zucchini lengthwise, creating fettuccini-like strips. After each peel, rotate the zucchini clockwise slightly before each new peel. Continue peeling until you reach the core with the seeds; discard the core. Repeat with remaining zucchini.

Bring 1 gallon water to a boil over high heat. Add the zucchini ribbons and cook for 1 minute. Remove the zucchini using tongs and place in a colander filled with ice. Allow to cool for 5 minutes. Drain any remaining liquid, discard the ice, and place the zucchini ribbons in a medium bowl. Cut the bell pepper into ½-inch strips, then slice the strips in half. Toss the bell pepper with the zucchini ribbons.

In a blender, combine the roasted red peppers and yogurt. Blend until smooth, 2 minutes.

Add the yogurt-pepper sauce to the zucchini ribbons. Gently toss to evenly coat. Serve immediately.

SERVING SIZE: ½ cup

NUTRITION INFORMATION (PER SERVING): Calories: 33; Total Fat: 0 grams; Saturated Fat: 0 grams; Protein: 3 grams; Total Carbohydrates: 6 grams; Sugars: 2 grams; Fiber: 1 gram; Cholesterol: 0 milligrams; Sodium: 272 milligrams

Pasta Salad with Tomatoes, Peppers, and Olives

My kids love pasta salad, so one night I dressed mine with colorful summer vegetables to entice them. I was pleasantly surprised when all three of them requested leftovers to take to school for lunch the next day!

Prep time: 15 minutes *Cook time:* 12 minutes SERVES 8

- 8 ounces bow-tie pasta, preferably whole-grain
- 1 cup cherry tomatoes
- 1 medium orange or yellow bell pepper
- 1 medium cucumber
- ½ cup pitted canned black olives
- ¼ cup nonfat plain Greek yogurt
- ¼ cup light mayonnaise
- ½ teaspoon grated lemon zest
- ¼ teaspoon onion powder
- ⅛ teaspoon salt
- ⅛ teaspoon freshly ground black pepper

Bring 4 quarts water to a boil in a large pot over high heat. Add the pasta and cook, stirring occasionally, until al dente, about 12 minutes. Drain completely (do not rinse) and place in a large bowl.

While the pasta is cooking, halve the cherry tomatoes lengthwise. Cut the bell pepper in half, discard the seeds, and cut into ½-inch dice. Peel the cucumber and cut in half lengthwise, remove the seeds, and slice into half-moons. Halve the olives lengthwise.

In a small bowl, combine the yogurt, mayonnaise, lemon zest, onion powder, salt, and pepper. Add the yogurt mixture and the vegetables to the pasta and toss to evenly coat.

SERVING SIZE: 1 cup

NUTRITION INFORMATION (PER SERVING): Calories: 161; Total Fat: 4 grams; Saturated Fat: 0 grams; Protein: 5 grams; Total Carbohydrates: 25 grams; Sugars: 3 grams; Fiber: 2 grams; Cholesterol: 3 milligrams; Sodium: 153 milligrams

Broccoli Slaw with Cranberries

Slaws drowning in buckets of mayo are not very healthy or appetizing. I prefer when the natural flavor of the ingredients can shine through. This broccoli slaw is the perfect example, with fresh broccoli, edamame, carrots, and pumpkin and sunflower seeds. You can taste each in every scrumptious bite.

Prep time: 20 minutes, plus 2 hours refrigeration *Cook time:* 0 minutes SERVES 6

FOR SALAD

1 cup frozen shelled edamame
1½ pounds fresh broccoli
4 medium carrots, peeled and grated (1 cup)
½ cup dried cranberries
½ cup unsalted shelled pumpkin seeds
¼ cup unsalted shelled sunflower seeds

FOR DRESSING

½ cup nonfat plain Greek yogurt
3 tablespoons light mayonnaise
2 tablespoons apple cider vinegar
⅛ teaspoon salt
⅛ teaspoon freshly ground black pepper

To make the salad: Fill a medium pot with water and bring it to a boil over high heat. Add the edamame and lower the heat to medium. Cook for about 5 minutes, until heated through. Drain, and set aside to cool for 5 minutes.

Cut the broccoli florets from the head. Thinly slice the broccoli stems and florets, using a chef's knife or mandoline.

In a large bowl, combine the edamame, sliced broccoli, grated carrots, cranberries, pumpkin seeds, and sunflower seeds.

Prepare the dressing: In a small bowl, mix together the yogurt, mayonnaise, vinegar, salt, and pepper.

Pour the dressing over the ingredients in the bowl and toss to combine. Cover the bowl with plastic wrap and refrigerate for at least 2 hours before serving. The slaw will keep, covered, in the refrigerator for up to 3 days.

SERVING SIZE: 1½ cups

NUTRITION INFORMATION (PER SERVING): Calories: 237; Total Fat: 12 grams; Saturated Fat: 2 grams; Protein: 12 grams; Total Carbohydrates: 24 grams; Sugars: 12 grams; Fiber: 7 grams; Cholesterol: 0 milligrams; Sodium: 159 milligrams

Rosemary Olive Bread

My dad always had a weakness for freshly baked bread. Any time we would pass by a bakery, he would find an excuse to pick up a warm loaf. The olive loaf quickly became a family favorite, devoured in less than 5 minutes by my siblings and me. Every time I bake this bread, the delicious smell wafting through my kitchen brings back those wonderful family memories.

Prep time: 15 minutes *Cook time:* 40 minutes SERVES 10

- Cooking spray
- 2¼ cups unbleached all-purpose flour
- 2 teaspoons baking powder
- ½ teaspoon baking soda
- 1 teaspoon salt
- 4 ounces pitted canned black olives, coarsely chopped (1 cup)
- 1 tablespoon chopped fresh rosemary leaves
- ¾ cup nonfat plain Greek yogurt
- ½ cup low-fat milk
- 2 large eggs
- 2 tablespoons canola oil

Preheat the oven to 400°F. Coat an 8-inch loaf pan with cooking spray and set it aside.

In a large bowl, sift together the flour, baking powder, baking soda, and salt. Stir in the chopped olives and rosemary until thoroughly incorporated.

In a medium bowl, combine the yogurt, milk, eggs, and canola oil. Stir until the mixture is thick, with a buttermilk-like consistency.

Make a well in the center of the dry ingredients and pour in the wet ingredients. Stir with as few strokes as possible until all the ingredients are just mixed. Pour the batter into the prepared loaf pan, and smooth the top with the back of a spoon. Bake on the center rack in the oven until a toothpick inserted in the center of the bread comes out clean, 40 minutes.

SERVING SIZE: 1 (¾-inch) slice

NUTRITION INFORMATION (PER SERVING): Calories: 163; Total Fat: 6 grams; Saturated Fat: 1 gram; Protein: 6 grams; Total Carbohydrates: 22 grams; Sugars: 2 grams; Fiber: 0 grams; Cholesterol: 38 milligrams; Sodium: 512 milligrams

Fresh herbs are low in calories but high in nutrition and health benefits. One tablespoon of fresh rosemary has 2 calories along with vitamin A, vitamin C, iron, and manganese. It also has several plant chemicals, like the antioxidant rosmarinic acid, shown to help decrease inflammation and help protect against various forms of cancer.

CHAPTER 7

Desserts

Banana-Strawberry Crepes with Dark Chocolate Drizzle

On a recent visit to Paris, I ordered a decadent crepe filled with bananas and chocolate. It was so unbelievably delicious that I was determined to re-create that memory by concocting a similar dessert that was equally mouthwatering without the calorie overload. Mission accomplished!

Prep time: 20 minutes *Cook time:* 20 minutes SERVES 8

1¼ cups reduced-fat milk
4 large egg whites
1 tablespoon canola oil
1 cup unbleached all-purpose flour
Cooking spray
2 ounces dark chocolate (60% to 70% cocoa)
2 medium bananas
1½ cups nonfat strawberry Greek yogurt

In a medium bowl, whisk together the milk, egg whites, canola oil, and ¾ cup water. Gradually whisk in the flour until the mixture is well combined.

Coat a large skillet with cooking spray and heat it over medium heat. Ladle ⅓ cup of the batter into the skillet and cook, without moving it, until the edges begin to brown, about 1½ minutes. Using a spatula, flip the crepe over and cook for 20 seconds. Then transfer the crepe to a large plate. Repeat with the remaining batter, placing parchment paper between the crepes to prevent sticking, to make 8 crepes.

In a small bowl, melt the chocolate in the microwave, about 1 minute, stirring halfway through. Set aside to cool slightly.

Thinly slice the bananas. In a medium bowl, fold the bananas into the yogurt.

To assemble, place 1 crepe on a large plate and spoon ¼ cup of the banana-yogurt mixture over it. Fold both sides in to seal, and turn the crepe over so the seam is on the bottom. Drizzle

Cocoa beans contain good-for-you nutrients like vitamin A, vitamin E, several B vitamins, calcium, iron, and potassium. Cocoa is also brimming with more antioxidants than green tea or red wine! In order to reap these benefits, choose dark chocolate labeled 60% to 70% cocoa.

1 teaspoon of the melted chocolate over the top. Repeat with the remainder of the crepes, and serve.

SERVING SIZE: 1 crepe and 1 teaspoon melted chocolate

NUTRITION INFORMATION (PER SERVING): Calories: 198; Total Fat: 5 grams; Saturated Fat: 2 grams; Protein: 9 grams; Total Carbohydrates: 29 grams; Sugars: 11 grams; Fiber: 2 grams; Cholesterol: 3 milligrams; Sodium: 72 milligrams

Plum Clafoutis

French desserts have a reputation for being outlandishly high in calories and fat. But now you can enjoy one without the guilt. This classic custard-like French treat takes minutes to assemble, though it may seem to everyone else that you slaved over a hot stove for a long while.

Prep time: 15 minutes *Cook time:* 1 hour SERVES 8

- Cooking spray
- 5 large eggs
- ¾ cup granulated sugar
- ¾ cup nonfat plain Greek yogurt
- 1 cup reduced-fat milk
- 2 teaspoons vanilla extract
- 1 tablespoon orange-flavored liqueur (I like Grand Marnier; optional)
- ¾ cup unbleached all-purpose flour
- ⅛ teaspoon salt
- 1 pound (about 4) plums, pitted and sliced
- 1 tablespoon unsifted confectioners' sugar

Preheat the oven to 375°F. Coat an 8-inch pie dish with cooking spray and set it aside.

In a large bowl, whisk together the eggs, sugar, yogurt, milk, vanilla extract, and orange liqueur (if using). In a medium bowl, sift together the flour and salt. Add the flour mixture to the egg mixture and stir until thoroughly combined.

Pour the batter into the prepared pie dish. Arrange the plum slices over the batter, submerging them partially.

Bake on the center rack in the oven until the middle is puffy and golden brown and a toothpick inserted in the center comes out clean, 1 hour. Remove from the oven (the clafoutis will deflate).

Sprinkle with the confectioners' sugar just before serving. Cut into 8 slices and serve warm.

SERVING SIZE: 1 slice

NUTRITION INFORMATION (PER SERVING): Calories: 216; Total Fat: 4 grams; Saturated Fat: 1 gram; Protein: 9 grams; Total Carbohydrates: 37 grams; Sugars: 28 grams; Fiber: 1 gram; Cholesterol: 119 milligrams; Sodium: 109 milligrams

Toasted Almond-Apricot Cake

Unbelievably, there is no oil or butter in this cake. The moisture comes solely from the yogurt, milk, and eggs—making it low in fat and light on the palate.

Prep time: 20 minutes *Cook time:* 34 minutes SERVES 20

- Cooking spray
- ¾ cup nonfat plain Greek yogurt
- ¼ cup low-fat milk
- ¾ cup granulated sugar
- 3 large eggs, beaten
- 1 teaspoon pure almond extract
- 1 teaspoon vanilla extract
- ½ cup almond flour
- 1¾ cups unbleached all-purpose flour
- 1 teaspoon baking powder
- 1 teaspoon baking soda
- ½ teaspoon salt
- 3 or 4 fresh apricots (about 8 ounces), pitted and sliced

Preheat the oven to 350°F. Coat an 8 x 11-inch baking dish with cooking spray and set it aside.

In a large bowl, combine the yogurt, milk, sugar, eggs, and almond and vanilla extracts. Stir until thoroughly combined. Set aside.

Sprinkle the almond flour into a medium skillet and carefully toast it over medium heat until aromatic, stirring occasionally, 3 to 4 minutes. Then transfer the almond flour to a large bowl and add the all-purpose flour, baking powder, baking soda, and salt. Stir to combine.

Pour the flour mixture into the yogurt mixture, stirring swiftly to combine and taking care not to overmix. Spoon the batter into the prepared baking dish, and spread it out evenly with the back of a spoon or spatula. Arrange the apricot slices on top of the batter. Place the baking dish on the center rack in the oven and bake until the cake is golden and springy to the touch, about 30 minutes. Remove from the oven and let the cake cool for at least 10 minutes; then cut it into roughly 2-inch squares.

SERVING SIZE: 1 (2-inch) square

NUTRITION INFORMATION (PER SERVING): Calories: 103; Total Fat: 2 grams; Saturated Fat: 0 grams; Protein: 4 grams; Total Carbohydrates: 18 grams; Sugars: 9 grams; Fiber: 1 gram; Cholesterol: 28 milligrams; Sodium: 163 milligrams

Double Chocolate Chip Cookies

One of my all-time favorite sweets is chocolate chip cookies, especially the chewy kind—but the calories are typically through the roof. Luckily, Greek yogurt can easily be used in place of most of the butter. The result is finger-licking-good chocolate chip cookies without the guilt.

Prep time: 20 minutes *Cook time:* 12 to 15 minutes

MAKES 30 COOKIES

- Cooking spray
- 1 cup unbleached all-purpose flour
- 1 cup whole wheat pastry flour
- ¼ cup unsweetened cocoa powder
- 1 teaspoon baking powder
- ⅛ teaspoon kosher salt
- ¼ cup (½ stick) unsalted butter, melted
- 6 tablespoons nonfat plain Greek yogurt
- 1 cup packed light brown sugar
- ½ cup granulated sugar
- 1 teaspoon vanilla extract
- 2 large eggs
- ¾ cup semisweet chocolate chips

Preheat the oven to 350°F. Coat a baking sheet with cooking spray and set it aside.

In a medium bowl, sift together the all-purpose flour, pastry flour, cocoa powder, baking powder, and salt.

In a large bowl, whisk together the melted butter and the yogurt. Stir in the brown sugar, granulated sugar, and vanilla extract. Add the eggs, one at a time, whisking until incorporated. Slowly add the dry ingredients to the wet, folding gently to combine. Fold in the chocolate chips, distributing them evenly throughout the dough.

Scoop up 1 heaping tablespoon of the dough, and using your hands, roll it into a ball. Place it on the prepared baking sheet. Repeat with the remaining dough, leaving about 1 inch between cookies. Bake until the cookies are soft to the touch but not mushy, 12 to 15 minutes. Remove the baking sheet from the oven and allow the cookies to cool for 5 minutes, then transfer to a wire rack to cool for an additional 10 minutes before serving.

SERVING SIZE: 1 cookie

NUTRITION INFORMATION (PER SERVING): Calories: 113; Total Fat: 3 grams; Saturated Fat: 2 grams; Protein: 2 grams; Total Carbohydrates: 20 grams; Sugars: 13 grams; Fiber: 1 gram; Cholesterol: 16 milligrams; Sodium: 27 milligrams

Tropical Island Ice Pops

When my daughter was six, she came home from school one day to inform me that three of her kindergarten friends wanted to come over to play. Seems she had told her classmates about the fabulous ice pops her mom "the nutritionist" had made and they all wanted a taste!

Prep time: 10 minutes, plus 4 hours in the freezer *Cook time:* 0 minutes MAKES 12 POPSICLES

- 1½ cups vanilla coconut milk
- 1½ cups fresh or frozen mango chunks
- ½ cup nonfat vanilla Greek yogurt
- ½ cup unsweetened shredded coconut
- 1 large ripe banana

Place the coconut milk, mango, yogurt, shredded coconut, and banana in a blender or food processor and blend until completely combined and smooth, about 1 minute.

Pour into 12 standard ice pop molds, using a ¼-cup scoop, and insert a popsicle stick into each one. Freeze until set, at least 4 hours.

SERVING SIZE: 1 popsicle

NUTRITION INFORMATION (PER SERVING): Calories: 52; Total Fat: 2 grams; Saturated Fat: 2 grams; Protein: 1 gram; Total Carbohydrates: 8 grams; Sugars: 6 grams; Fiber: 1 gram; Cholesterol: 0 milligrams; Sodium: 10 milligrams

To remove a popsicle from its mold, you may need to hold the mold under warm running water for 30 seconds.

Lemon Panna Cotta with Orange-Thyme Sauce

There is no heavy cream in this delicious rendition of the popular dessert. The balance of the lemon, orange, thyme, and vanilla enhances the tantalizing flavor—and the 220 calories and just 1 gram of fat per serving will please your waistline.

Prep time: 15 minutes, plus 4 hours refrigeration *Cook time:* 10 minutes SERVES 4

FOR PANNA COTTA

2 cups nonfat lemon Greek yogurt
¼ cup unsifted confectioners' sugar
2 teaspoons grated lemon zest
¾ cup reduced-fat milk
2 teaspoons unflavored gelatin powder

FOR ORANGE-THYME SAUCE

2 tablespoons honey
½ teaspoon vanilla extract
5 sprigs fresh thyme
4 strips orange zest
2 oranges, peeled and segmented, pith removed

To make the panna cotta: Stir together the lemon yogurt, confectioners' sugar, and lemon zest in a medium bowl. Set aside and allow the mixture to come to room temperature, about 20 minutes.

Meanwhile, pour the milk into a small saucepan off the stove, and sprinkle the gelatin over it. Set aside to allow the gelatin to soften, 5 minutes. Then place the pan over low heat to warm the milk and melt the gelatin, being careful not to let it boil. Stir until the gelatin has melted, 1 to 2 minutes. Then stir the warm milk into the yogurt mixture and combine thoroughly.

Pour approximately ½ cup of the mixture into each of four ramekins or small bowls. Cover with plastic wrap and chill in the refrigerator for at least 4 hours or up to 12 hours.

To make the orange-thyme sauce: Pour ½ cup water into a small saucepan, and stir in the honey, vanilla extract, thyme sprigs, and orange zest. Bring to a boil over high heat; then remove from the heat and let steep for 5 minutes. Discard the thyme and orange zest, and allow the sauce to cool for another 5 minutes. Then cut the orange segments into thirds, add them to the sauce, and toss to coat evenly.

Remove the ramekins from the refrigerator, top each one with 2 tablespoons of the orange-thyme sauce, and serve.

SERVING SIZE: 1 panna cotta and 2 tablespoons sauce

NUTRITION INFORMATION (PER SERVING): Calories: 220; Total Fat: 1 gram; Saturated Fat: 1 gram; Protein: 14 grams; Total Carbohydrates: 41 grams; Sugars: 36 grams; Fiber: 2 grams; Cholesterol: 5 milligrams; Sodium: 87 milligrams

Italian-Style Cheesecake Dip with Strawberries

My husband's favorite dessert is cheesecake. He can devour a 1,200-calorie piece in a flash! I quickly learned that this quick and easy dip can satisfy his sweet tooth just the same—and for a fraction of the calories.

Prep time: 10 minutes *Cook time:* 0 minutes SERVES 4

- 2 graham crackers
- 1 (5.3-ounce) container nonfat honey Greek yogurt
- ½ cup whipped cream cheese
- ¼ cup part-skim ricotta cheese
- 20 medium-size fresh strawberries

Place the graham crackers in a food processer and process until fine. In a small bowl, stir together the yogurt, cream cheese, and ricotta. Fold in the graham cracker crumbs.

Place the cheesecake dip in a serving dish, cover it with plastic wrap, and chill in the refrigerator for at least 30 minutes or up to 3 days. Serve with the fresh strawberries.

SERVING SIZE: ¼ cup dip and 5 strawberries

NUTRITION INFORMATION (PER SERVING): Calories: 146; Total Fat: 8 grams; Saturated Fat: 4 grams; Protein: 7 grams; Total Carbohydrates: 14 grams; Sugars: 9 grams; Fiber: 1 gram; Cholesterol: 25 milligrams; Sodium: 138 milligrams

Choose strawberries that are bright red in color, and be sure to examine the bottom of the container for soft, bruised, or moldy berries. Always rinse strawberries just before eating; pre-washing can cause them to mold quickly. Store fresh strawberries in the refrigerator for up to 3 days.

Pineapple-Coconut Trifle

Angel food cake is made with egg whites and is free of fat. It provides a light and airy mouthfeel to this trifle while layers of sweet pineapple sauce and toasted coconut and pecans add a burst of flavor. Impress guests at your next shindig or bring it to a potluck affair.

Prep time: 20 minutes, plus 1 hour refrigeration *Cook time:* 16 minutes SERVES 8

1 medium pineapple
1 tablespoon unsalted butter
⅓ cup packed dark brown sugar
1 cup raw pecans, chopped
¾ cup unsweetened shredded coconut
2 cups nonfat plain Greek yogurt
1 (10-ounce) store-bought angel food cake, cut into 1-inch cubes

Slice the top off the pineapple, and then cut off all the skin. Quarter the pineapple lengthwise, remove the core, and cut into 1-inch dice.

Melt the butter in a medium saucepan over medium heat. Add the pineapple and the brown sugar and cook, stirring occasionally, until the pineapple juice and sugar develop into a caramel-like sauce, about 10 minutes. Remove the pan from the heat and set aside to cool for about 5 minutes.

In a medium saucepan, toast ⅓ cup of the chopped pecans over low heat until browned, about 3 minutes. Remove the pecans from the pan and set them aside to cool for about 10 minutes.

Meanwhile, in the same saucepan, combine the remaining chopped pecans and the coconut. Toast over low heat until browned, about 3 minutes. Then remove the pan from the heat and set aside to cool, about 10 minutes.

Place the yogurt in a medium bowl, and gently fold in the pecan-coconut mixture.

In a trifle dish or a large glass serving bowl, arrange half the cubed angel food cake in an even layer. Top with 1 cup of the yogurt mixture and about 2½ cups of the cooked pineapple (with sauce). Repeat the layers of cake, yogurt mixture, and pineapple, and then top with the reserved ⅓ cup toasted pecans. Cover the bowl with plastic wrap and chill in the refrigerator for at least 1 hour before serving.

SERVING SIZE: ⅛ trifle

NUTRITION INFORMATION (PER SERVING): Calories: 350; Total Fat: 16 grams; Saturated Fat: 6 grams; Protein: 10 grams; Total Carbohydrates: 48 grams; Sugars: 21 grams; Fiber: 4 grams; Cholesterol: 4 milligrams; Sodium: 288 milligrams

Rice Pudding with Drunken Cherry Sauce

This grown-up version of rice pudding combines traditional flavors with a sophisticated sauce. The pudding is reminiscent of many child-friendly versions with honey, vanilla, cinnamon, and nutmeg, but then it's topped with a cherry sauce infused with cinnamon and Grand Marnier. Yum!

Prep time: 15 minutes, plus 1 hour refrigeration *Cook time:* 50 minutes SERVES 4

FOR RICE PUDDING

¾ cup Arborio rice

3½ cups low-fat milk

1 tablespoon honey

¼ teaspoon salt

1 (5.3-ounce) container nonfat vanilla Greek yogurt

¼ teaspoon ground cinnamon

⅛ teaspoon ground nutmeg

FOR DRUNKEN CHERRY SAUCE

6 ounces fresh or frozen pitted cherries (thawed if frozen)

1 tablespoon honey

1 cinnamon stick

1 tablespoon Grand Marnier

To make the rice pudding: Combine the rice, 3 cups of the milk, the honey, and the salt in a medium saucepan. Bring to a boil over medium heat; then lower the heat and simmer, uncovered, stirring occasionally, until the rice is tender and most of the liquid has been absorbed, about 35 minutes. Add the remaining ½ cup milk and bring the mixture back to a boil over medium-high heat. Lower the heat again and simmer until most of the liquid has been absorbed, 10 minutes. Remove the saucepan from the heat and set aside to cool for 5 minutes. Then fold in the yogurt, cinnamon, and nutmeg. Place the pudding in a medium bowl, cover with plastic wrap, and chill in the refrigerator for at least 1 hour and up to 3 days.

To make the drunken cherry sauce: Put half of the cherries, ¼ cup water, and the honey in a blender or food processor and puree until smooth. Transfer the puree to a clean saucepan and add the cinnamon stick. Bring to a boil over high heat; then reduce the heat and simmer for 3 minutes. Remove the pan from the heat and discard the cinnamon stick. Dice the remaining cherries into small pieces and add them to the sauce. Stir in the Grand

Marnier. Allow the sauce to cool for at least 10 minutes. The sauce can be served immediately or stored, covered, in the refrigerator for up to 3 days.

To serve, place ½ cup of the rice pudding in each of four small bowls and top each with 2 tablespoons of the sauce.

SERVING SIZE: ½ cup pudding and 2 tablespoons sauce

NUTRITION INFORMATION (PER SERVING): Calories: 325; Total Fat: 2 grams; Saturated Fat: 1 gram; Protein: 16 grams; Total Carbohydrates: 60 grams; Sugars: 31 grams; Fiber: 1 gram; Cholesterol: 9 milligrams; Sodium: 303 milligrams

Layered Carrot Cake with Cream Cheese Frosting

Two layers of moist cake packed with a pound of shredded carrots, flavored with cinnamon, nutmeg, and ginger and topped with a scrumptious cream cheese frosting—all for around 250 calories a slice. Yes, it is possible!

Prep time: 30 minutes *Cook time:* 22 to 27 minutes SERVES 12

FOR CAKE

Cooking spray
1¼ cups unbleached all-purpose flour
1¼ cups whole wheat pastry flour
1½ teaspoons ground cinnamon
1 teaspoon ground nutmeg
1 teaspoon ground ginger
1 teaspoon baking powder
½ teaspoon baking soda
⅛ teaspoon kosher salt
1 cup low-fat milk
¾ cup packed light brown sugar
½ cup (1 stick) unsalted butter, melted
¼ cup nonfat plain Greek yogurt
3 large eggs
1 tablespoon vanilla extract
5 to 6 large carrots (about 1 pound), peeled and grated

FOR FROSTING

¾ cup whipped cream cheese
2 tablespoons nonfat plain Greek yogurt
1 teaspoon vanilla extract
2 tablespoons unsifted confectioners' sugar

Preheat the oven to 350°F. Coat two 9-inch round cake pans with cooking spray and set them aside.

In a medium bowl, sift together the all-purpose flour, pastry flour, cinnamon, nutmeg, ginger, baking powder, baking soda, and salt.

In a large bowl, whisk together the milk, brown sugar, melted butter, and yogurt until smooth. Add the eggs and vanilla extract, and whisk to combine. Slowly add the flour mixture to the wet mixture and stir to combine. Then add the shredded carrots and fold in to incorporate.

Divide the batter evenly between the prepared cake pans. Bake on the center rack in the oven until a toothpick inserted into the center of each cake comes out clean, 22 to

27 minutes. Remove the pans from the oven and set aside to cool for 5 minutes. Then remove the cakes from the pans and let them cool on a wire rack for at least 15 minutes.

Meanwhile, prepare the frosting: In a small bowl, combine the cream cheese, yogurt, vanilla extract, and confectioners' sugar.

To assemble the cake, frost the top of one cake layer with half of the frosting, spreading it evenly over the top with a spatula. Top with the second cake layer, and evenly spread the remaining frosting over the top with a spatula.

Serve immediately or store, covered, in the refrigerator for up to 5 days.

SERVING SIZE: 1 slice (1⁄12 of cake)

NUTRITION INFORMATION (PER SERVING): Calories: 288; Total Fat: 12 grams; Saturated Fat: 8 grams; Protein: 7 grams; Total Carbohydrates: 38 grams; Sugars: 17 grams; Fiber: 3 grams; Cholesterol: 77 milligrams; Sodium: 221 milligrams

Vanilla-Lover Cupcakes

The vanilla versus chocolate debate is never-ending at my house. My son and husband love chocolate, while my girls prefer vanilla. These genuine vanilla cupcakes are to honor my daughters—hard-core vanilla lovers!

Prep time: 20 minutes *Cook time:* 25 minutes MAKES 12 CUPCAKES

FOR CUPCAKES

1¼ cups unbleached all-purpose flour
1 cup whole wheat pastry flour
1 teaspoon baking powder
½ teaspoon baking soda
¼ teaspoon kosher salt
¼ cup (½ stick) unsalted butter, melted
¼ cup unsweetened applesauce
¼ cup nonfat vanilla Greek yogurt
¾ cup granulated sugar
1 cup low-fat milk
3 large eggs
1 teaspoon vanilla extract

FOR VANILLA BEAN FROSTING

½ cup heavy whipping cream
2 tablespoons granulated sugar
2 whole vanilla beans
12 fresh raspberries, for garnish

Preheat the oven to 350°F. Insert paper liners in a 12-cup cupcake tin and set it aside.

In a medium bowl, sift together the all-purpose flour, pastry flour, baking powder, baking soda, and salt.

In a large bowl, whisk together the melted butter, applesauce, and yogurt. Add the sugar and stir to combine. Add the milk. Then add the eggs, one at a time, whisking until each one is incorporated into the batter. Stir in the vanilla extract.

Slowly add the dry ingredients to the wet, folding gently until completely combined. Scoop a heaping ¼ cup of the batter into each cupcake liner. Gently tap the tin against the counter several times to remove any air bubbles.

Place the tin in the oven and bake until a toothpick inserted in the center of a cupcake comes out clean, about 25 minutes. Remove the tin from the oven and set it aside to cool for 5 minutes; then transfer the cupcakes to a wire rack to cool completely.

Vanilla beans tend to be expensive, especially if you purchase them at a specialty store. You can find better prices online or sometimes at your local supermarket.

Meanwhile, to make the vanilla bean frosting: Combine the whipping cream and sugar in a medium bowl. On a cutting board, split the vanilla beans in half lengthwise. Then, using the tip of the knife, carefully scrape out the seeds and add them to the cream. Using an electric stand mixer or handheld mixer, whip until stiff peaks form, about 5 minutes.

Top each cooled cupcake with 1 tablespoon of the whipped cream frosting and garnish with a raspberry. Serve immediately, or store in an airtight container in the refrigerator for up to 3 days.

SERVING SIZE: 1 cupcake with 1 tablespoon frosting and 1 raspberry

NUTRITION INFORMATION (PER SERVING): Calories: 230; Total Fat: 9 grams; Saturated Fat: 6 grams; Protein: 5 grams; Total Carbohydrates: 33 grams; Sugars: 17 grams; Fiber: 1 gram; Cholesterol: 71 milligrams; Sodium: 173 milligrams

Peaches and Cream

Nothing beats juicy peaches on a hot summer day. Luckily, it doesn't have to be summer for you to enjoy the goodness of this stone fruit. If fresh is out of season, store unsweetened slices in the freezer and grab your grill pan. You're in for a delightful treat any time of the year.

Prep time: 10 minutes *Cook time:* 5 minutes SERVES 4

- 2 tablespoons canola oil
- 1 teaspoon ground cinnamon
- ⅛ teaspoon ground nutmeg
- 1 pound frozen sliced peaches, thawed (4 cups)
- 1 cup nonfat vanilla Greek yogurt
- 1 tablespoon pure maple syrup

Preheat a grill pan over medium heat.

In a medium bowl, whisk together the canola oil, cinnamon, and nutmeg. Add the peaches and toss to coat evenly. Then place the peaches on the grill pan and cook until lightly browned, about 5 minutes. Remove the pan from the heat and allow to cool for about 5 minutes.

In a small bowl, combine the yogurt and maple syrup.

To serve, place ¾ cup grilled peaches into each of four small bowls and top with ¼ cup of the yogurt mixture.

SERVING SIZE: 1 bowl

NUTRITION INFORMATION (PER SERVING): Calories: 157; Total Fat: 7 grams; Saturated Fat: 1 gram; Protein: 6 grams; Total Carbohydrates: 20 grams; Sugars: 16 grams; Fiber: 2 grams; Cholesterol: 0 milligrams; Sodium: 24 milligrams

Dirty Blondies

Why are these blondies "dirty"? I used oat bran to replace part of the flour to add fiber, iron, and quite a few B vitamins. One evening as I was preparing a batch and measuring out the oat bran, one of my daughters asked if my batter was a bowlful of delicious dirt! The name just stuck.

Prep time: 20 minutes *Cook time:* 45 minutes

MAKES 16 BLONDIES

- Cooking spray
- 2 cups unbleached all-purpose flour
- ¼ cup oat bran
- 1 teaspoon baking soda
- ⅛ teaspoon kosher salt
- ½ cup (1 stick) unsalted butter, melted
- ¼ cup nonfat plain Greek yogurt
- 1 cup packed dark brown sugar
- ½ cup granulated sugar
- 3 large eggs
- 1 teaspoon vanilla extract
- ¾ cup semisweet chocolate chips
- ⅓ cup chopped raw walnuts

Preheat the oven to 350°F. Coat an 8 x 8-inch baking dish with cooking spray and set it aside.

In a medium bowl, sift together the flour, oat bran, baking soda, and salt.

In a large bowl, whisk together the melted butter and the yogurt. Add the brown sugar and granulated sugar, stirring until smooth. Whisk in the eggs, one at a time. Add the vanilla extract and stir to combine. Slowly add the dry ingredients to the wet, folding gently to combine. Fold in the chocolate chips and walnuts, distributing them evenly throughout the batter.

Spoon the batter into the prepared baking dish and smooth the top evenly with a spatula. Bake until the top is golden brown and a toothpick inserted in the center comes out clean, 45 minutes. Remove the pan from the oven and allow the blondies to cool for at least 10 minutes before cutting into 2 x 2-inch pieces and serving.

SERVING SIZE: 1 (2-inch) square

NUTRITION INFORMATION (PER SERVING): Calories: 255; Total Fat: 11 grams; Saturated Fat: 6 grams; Protein: 4 grams; Total Carbohydrates: 38 grams; Sugars: 25 grams; Fiber: 1 gram; Cholesterol: 50 milligrams; Sodium: 111 milligrams

Trail Mix Cookies

You will find all the good-for-you ingredients from a trail mix packed into this moist cookie—the oats, raisins, and sunflower seeds contain fiber that will keep you satisfied. It is a dessert you can always feel good about.

Prep time: 20 minutes *Cook time:* 12 minutes

MAKES 40 COOKIES

- Cooking spray
- 1 cup unbleached all-purpose flour
- 1 teaspoon baking soda
- 1 teaspoon ground cinnamon
- ⅛ teaspoon kosher salt
- ½ cup (1 stick) unsalted butter, melted
- ¼ cup nonfat plain Greek yogurt
- 1 cup packed light brown sugar
- ½ cup granulated sugar
- 2 large eggs
- 1 teaspoon vanilla extract
- 2 cups old-fashioned rolled oats
- 1 cup seedless golden raisins
- ⅓ cup unsalted shelled sunflower seeds

Preheat the oven to 350°F. Coat a baking sheet with cooking spray and set it aside.

In a medium bowl, sift together the flour, baking soda, cinnamon, and salt.

In a large bowl, whisk together the melted butter and yogurt. Add the brown sugar and granulated sugar and stir until smooth. Add the eggs, one at a time, whisking until each one is incorporated, and then add the vanilla extract. Whisk until the mixture is light brown and thoroughly combined.

Slowly add the dry ingredients to the wet, folding gently until combined. One ingredient at a time, fold in the oats, raisins, and sunflower seeds.

Scoop up 1 heaping tablespoon of the dough and drop it onto the prepared baking sheet. Repeat with the remaining dough, leaving about 2 inches between cookies. Bake until the cookies are golden brown and slightly firm to the touch, about 12 minutes. Remove from the oven and allow to cool for 5 minutes, then transfer to a wire rack to finish cooling for at least 10 minutes before serving.

SERVING SIZE: 1 cookie

NUTRITION INFORMATION (PER SERVING): Calories: 97; Total Fat: 3 grams; Saturated Fat: 2 grams; Protein: 2 grams; Total Carbohydrates: 16 grams; Sugars: 10 grams; Fiber: 1 gram; Cholesterol: 15 milligrams; Sodium: 45 milligrams

Peach, Plum, and Apricot Pizza

When I first showed my fruit pizza to my kids, they all looked slightly confused. I explained that in many cultures, cheese is enjoyed alongside fruit for dessert—so why not layer them both on top of pizza dough!

Prep time: 10 minutes *Cook time:* 12 to 15 minutes SERVES 8

- Cooking spray
- 1 pound refrigerated pizza dough, at room temperature
- Unbleached all-purpose flour, for dusting
- 2 tablespoons unsalted butter
- 1 tablespoon granulated sugar
- 1 teaspoon ground cinnamon
- ¾ cup part-skim ricotta cheese
- ¼ cup nonfat plain Greek yogurt
- 1 medium peach
- 2 medium plums
- 1 apricot
- 1 tablespoon honey

Preheat the oven to 425°F. Coat a pizza pan or baking sheet with cooking spray and set it aside.

Roll out the pizza dough on a lightly floured surface to form a 14-inch round, and place it on the prepared pan. In a small saucepan, melt the butter over low heat. Add the sugar and cinnamon, and stir until combined. Brush this mixture over the pizza dough, and bake on the center rack in the oven until the crust is browned and the top is crisp, 12 to 15 minutes. Remove the pan from the oven and place it on a wire rack to cool for about 10 minutes.

Meanwhile, in a medium bowl, stir together the ricotta and yogurt. Wash, pit, and slice the peach and the plums into 16 pieces each. Wash, pit, and slice the apricot into 8 pieces. Place the pizza crust on a serving plate. Spread the ricotta-yogurt mixture over the pizza crust, and top with the peach, plum, and apricot slices, spreading them around evenly. Drizzle with the honey. Cut into 8 slices and serve.

SERVING SIZE: 1 slice

NUTRITION INFORMATION (PER SERVING): Calories: 234; Total Fat: 6 grams; Saturated Fat: 4 grams; Protein: 8 grams; Total Carbohydrates: 37 grams; Sugars: 12 grams; Fiber: 1 gram; Cholesterol: 15 milligrams; Sodium: 442 milligrams

Honey is a wonderful addition to your repertoire of natural sweeteners. It contains B vitamins, iron, potassium, and zinc along with several antioxidants. As with any sweetener, use it in small amounts.

Coconut Panna Cotta with Mango-Lime Coulis

Calling all coconut lovers—have I found the perfect dessert for you! The custard in this delightful treat is made with unsweetened coconut milk and coconut flakes, and the mouth-puckering combination of mango, lime, and mint perfectly balances the flavor.

Prep time: 30 minutes, plus 4 hours refrigeration *Cook time:* 8 minutes SERVES 4

FOR PANNA COTTA

2 cups nonfat plain Greek yogurt
½ cup superfine or regular granulated sugar
1 teaspoon vanilla extract
¾ cup unsweetened coconut milk
2 teaspoons unflavored gelatin powder
⅓ cup unsweetened shredded coconut

FOR MANGO-LIME COULIS

2 tablespoons granulated sugar
2 tablespoons fresh mint leaves
1 cup diced fresh or frozen mango
1 teaspoon grated lime zest
2 teaspoons fresh lime juice
⅛ teaspoon salt

To make the panna cotta: Stir together the yogurt, sugar, and vanilla extract in a medium bowl. Set aside and allow the mixture to come to room temperature, about 15 minutes.

Meanwhile, pour the coconut milk into a small saucepan off the stove and sprinkle the gelatin over it. Set aside to allow the gelatin to soften, 5 minutes. Then place the pan over low heat to warm the milk and melt the gelatin, being sure not to let it boil. Stir until the gelatin has melted, 1 to 2 minutes. Then stir the warm milk into the yogurt mixture and combine thoroughly. Stir in the shredded coconut.

Pour about ¾ cup of the panna cotta mixture into each of four ramekins or small bowls. Cover with plastic wrap and chill in the refrigerator to set, at least 4 hours or up to 12 hours.

Mangos contain plant compounds called flavonoids, which are shown to help control blood pressure and may also help reduce the risk of stroke and heart disease.

To make the mango-lime coulis: Combine the sugar and 2 tablespoons water in a small saucepan and bring to a boil over high heat. Cook for 1 minute and immediately remove the pan from the heat. Add the mint leaves, being sure to submerge them. Steep for 15 minutes. Then remove and discard the mint leaves.

Place the mango, lime zest, lime juice, and salt in a food processor or blender, and puree until smooth. Add the mint syrup and puree until incorporated.

To assemble, remove the ramekins from the refrigerator and top each panna cotta with 2 tablespoons of the mango-lime coulis.

SERVING SIZE: 1 panna cotta and 2 tablespoons coulis

NUTRITION INFORMATION (PER SERVING): Calories: 320; Total Fat: 6 gram; Saturated Fat: 5 grams; Protein: 14 grams; Total Carbohydrates: 57 grams; Sugars: 55 grams; Fiber: 2 grams; Cholesterol: 0 milligrams; Sodium: 154 milligrams

Spiced Chocolate Cupcakes

Flavored chocolate is all the rage in the fine chocolate aisle, so I decided to capture the popular combination of spicy and sweet in a cupcake. The pairing of unsweetened cocoa powder with ancho chile powder creates a kick that doesn't overwhelm, and the cooling cream cheese frosting helps to soothe.

Prep time: 25 minutes *Cook time:* 20 to 25 minutes

MAKES 24 CUPCAKES

FOR CUPCAKES

1½ cups unbleached all-purpose flour
1 cup whole wheat pastry flour
¾ cup unsweetened cocoa powder
4 teaspoons ancho chile powder
1 teaspoon baking powder
½ teaspoon baking soda
⅛ teaspoon kosher salt
1 cup granulated sugar
¼ cup (½ stick) unsalted butter, melted
¼ cup nonfat plain Greek yogurt
¼ cup prune butter (I like Simon Fischer Lekvar)
1½ cups low-fat milk
4 large eggs
1½ teaspoons vanilla extract

FOR FROSTING AND GARNISH

¾ cup whipped cream cheese
½ cup nonfat vanilla Greek yogurt
2 tablespoons confectioners' sugar
1 teaspoon vanilla extract
¼ ounce dark chocolate (60% to 70% cocoa)

Preheat the oven to 350°F. Insert paper liners in a 24-cup cupcake tin and set it aside.

In a medium bowl, sift together the all-purpose flour, pastry flour, cocoa powder, chile powder, baking powder, baking soda, and salt.

Prune butter is a low-fat substitute for butter. If you can't find it at your local market, pick up jarred pureed prunes from the baby food aisle instead. They'll do the trick, too!

In a large bowl, whisk together the granulated sugar, melted butter, yogurt, and prune butter. Stir until smooth. Whisk in the milk. Add the eggs, one at a time, whisking until each one is incorporated, and then add the vanilla extract. Stir the mixture until well combined. Slowly add the dry ingredients to the wet, folding gently until completely combined.

Scoop a heaping ¼ cup of the batter into each cupcake liner. Gently tap the tin against the counter several times to remove any air bubbles.

Place on the center rack in the oven and bake until a toothpick inserted in the center of a cupcake comes out clean, 20 to 25 minutes. Remove the tin from the oven and set aside to cool for 5 minutes; then transfer the cupcakes to a wire rack to cool completely.

While the cupcakes are cooling, make the frosting: Place the cream cheese, yogurt, confectioners' sugar, and vanilla extract in a small bowl and whisk to combine.

Frost each completely cooled cupcake with 1 tablespoon of the cream cheese frosting. Grate the dark chocolate over the frosting to garnish. Serve immediately or store in an airtight container in the refrigerator for up to 5 days.

SERVING SIZE: 1 cupcake with 1 tablespoon frosting and garnish

NUTRITION INFORMATION (PER SERVING): Calories: 153; Total Fat: 5 grams; Saturated Fat: 2 grams; Protein: 5 grams; Total Carbohydrates: 23 grams; Sugars: 11 grams; Fiber: 1 gram; Cholesterol: 42 milligrams; Sodium: 128 milligrams

Ice Cream Sandwiches with Pomegranate

These flavorful ice cream sandwiches are fun to make with the entire family. Replacing some of the vanilla ice cream with tangy nonfat Greek yogurt cuts out some of the unwanted fat and calories, while the pomegranate seeds give it a gorgeous hue and a yummy flavor.

Prep time: 30 minutes, plus 1 hour refrigeration *Cook time:* 0 minutes SERVES 6

- 1 cup regular vanilla ice cream (I like Turkey Hill)
- ½ cup nonfat plain Greek yogurt
- 3 tablespoons pomegranate seeds
- 6 graham cracker sheets
- ¾ ounce dark chocolate (60% to 70% cocoa)

Remove the ice cream from the freezer and allow it to sit at room temperature until it softens, about 10 minutes.

In a medium bowl, stir together the softened ice cream, yogurt, and pomegranate seeds. Place the mixture in a flat square dish or rimmed baking sheet, smoothing the top. Place in the freezer to harden, about 1 hour.

Break the graham cracker sheets in half, forming 12 squares. Grate the dark chocolate into a shallow bowl. Cut the ice cream into 6 equal squares. To assemble, sandwich each ice cream square between 2 graham cracker squares. Dip all sides of each sandwich into the grated chocolate, covering the ice cream. Serve immediately or put in an airtight container and freeze for later.

SERVING SIZE: 1 sandwich

NUTRITION INFORMATION (PER SERVING): Calories: 130; Total Fat: 5 grams; Saturated Fat: 2 grams; Protein: 4 grams; Total Carbohydrates: 19 grams; Sugars: 11 grams; Fiber: 1 gram; Cholesterol: 10 milligrams; Sodium: 92 milligrams

Peanut Butter–Banana Icebox Bars

Looking for a new, exciting, *and* healthy frozen treat? These icebox bars will do the trick. Frankly, flavorful peanut butter mixed with mashed bananas and vanilla-flavored Greek yogurt is pretty darn tasty on its own. Kick it up a notch and drizzle melted dark chocolate over the top. It is a decadent icy indulgence for under 125 calories!

Prep time: 15 minutes, plus 3 hours in the freezer *Cook time:* 15 minutes MAKES 16 BARS

- 8 graham cracker sheets
- 2 tablespoons unsalted butter
- 3 ripe bananas
- ½ cup natural creamy peanut butter
- 1 cup nonfat vanilla Greek yogurt
- ½ teaspoon vanilla extract
- 1 ounce dark chocolate (60% to 70% cocoa)

Preheat the oven to 350°F.

To make the crust, place the graham cracker sheets in a large resealable plastic bag and seal the bag. Using the bottom of a mixing bowl, a rolling pin, or your hands, crush the graham crackers into fine crumbs. Melt the butter in a medium bowl in the microwave, and then allow to cool for 1 to 2 minutes. Add the graham cracker crumbs to the melted butter and stir to combine. Pour the mixture into an 8 x 8-inch baking dish and spread it evenly over the bottom, pressing it gently into the corners. Bake until the crust is lightly browned, about 10 minutes. Remove the baking dish from the oven and set it aside to cool for about 10 minutes.

Meanwhile, mash the bananas in a small bowl. In a medium bowl, stir together the peanut butter, yogurt, and vanilla extract until combined. Add the mashed bananas and fold gently until thoroughly incorporated. Spoon the banana mixture over the cooled graham cracker crust. Place the baking dish in the freezer and chill until completely frozen, at least 3 hours.

Before serving, melt the chocolate in a small bowl in the microwave, about 1 minute, stirring halfway through. Remove the baking dish from the freezer and drizzle the melted chocolate over the top. Slice into 2 x 2-inch pieces and serve.

SERVING SIZE: 1 (2-inch) square

NUTRITION INFORMATION (PER SERVING): Calories: 124; Total Fat: 7 grams; Saturated Fat: 2 grams; Protein: 4 grams; Total Carbohydrates: 12 grams; Sugars: 6 grams; Fiber: 1 gram; Cholesterol: 4 milligrams; Sodium: 77 milligrams

Light and Dark Chocolate Brownies

Forget boxed brownies! This lightened double-dark-chocolate version is moist, chewy, and *beyond* delicious. I baked up a batch one rainy Saturday when my three brothers were in town. The only thing left after their visit was a trail of crumbs.

Prep time: 30 minutes *Cook time:* 27 minutes

MAKES 16 BROWNIES

- Cooking spray
- 3 ounces 60% dark chocolate
- ¼ cup (½ stick) unsalted butter, at room temperature
- ¾ cup unbleached all-purpose flour
- ⅓ cup unsweetened cocoa powder
- 1 teaspoon baking powder
- ¼ teaspoon kosher salt
- ¾ cup granulated sugar
- ¼ cup nonfat vanilla Greek yogurt
- 2 large eggs
- 1 teaspoon instant coffee powder
- 1 teaspoon vanilla extract
- ¼ cup mini dark chocolate chips

Preheat the oven to 350°F. Coat an 8 x 8-inch baking dish with cooking spray and set it aside.

Coarsely chop the dark chocolate. Place the chocolate and the butter in the top of a double boiler set over simmering water (see the box on page 42), and slowly melt, stirring until completely combined, about 5 minutes. Remove from the heat and set aside to cool for at least 5 minutes.

In a medium bowl, sift together the flour, cocoa powder, baking powder, and salt. Stir gently to combine.

In a separate medium bowl, whisk together the sugar and yogurt. Add the eggs, one at a time, whisking until each one is completely incorporated. Stir in the instant coffee powder and the vanilla extract. Slowly add the melted chocolate mixture, stirring until completely combined.

Add the dry ingredients to the wet and fold gently until combined. Fold in the chocolate chips.

Pour the batter into the prepared baking dish and spread it out evenly with a spatula.

Gently tap the dish against the counter several times to remove any air bubbles. Place the dish in the oven and bake until a toothpick inserted into the center comes out clean, about 22 minutes.

Remove the baking dish from the oven and allow the brownies to cool for about 10 minutes; then cut into 2-inch squares and serve.

SERVING SIZE: 1 (2-inch) square

NUTRITION INFORMATION (PER SERVING): Calories: 150; Total Fat: 7 grams; Saturated Fat: 4 grams; Protein: 2 grams; Total Carbohydrates: 20 grams; Sugars: 14 grams; Fiber: 1 gram; Cholesterol: 31 milligrams; Sodium: 78 milligrams

Coconut-Lemon Cookies

Sometimes it feels as though a compliment from my sister happens as often as winning the lottery. But after tasting every gluten-free cookie in New York City, she told me these were the best she'd ever had! They *must* be good.

Prep time: 25 minutes *Cook time:* 10 to 13 minutes MAKES 30 COOKIES

- Cooking spray
- 2 cups coconut flour
- ½ cup unsweetened shredded coconut
- ½ teaspoon baking soda
- ½ teaspoon baking powder
- ⅛ teaspoon kosher salt
- ½ cup blended nonfat lemon Greek yogurt
- ½ cup (1 stick) unsalted butter, melted
- ½ cup granulated sugar
- ½ cup packed light brown sugar
- 1 tablespoon grated lemon zest
- 3 large eggs
- 1 teaspoon vanilla extract

Preheat the oven to 350°F. Coat a baking sheet with cooking spray and set it aside.

In a medium bowl, combine the coconut flour, shredded coconut, baking soda, baking powder, and salt.

In a large bowl, whisk together the yogurt and melted butter until smooth. Stir in the granulated sugar, brown sugar, and lemon zest. Add the eggs, one at a time, whisking until each one is incorporated. Add the vanilla extract and whisk to combine. Slowly add the dry ingredients to the wet and fold gently to combine.

Scoop up 1 heaping tablespoon of the dough, and using wet hands, form it into a ball. Place it on the prepared baking sheet and repeat with the remaining dough, spacing the cookies 1 inch apart. Gently press down on the top of each one with the palm of your hand to flatten it. Bake on the center rack in the oven until the cookies are golden brown, 10 to 13 minutes. Remove the baking sheet from the oven and allow the cookies to cool for 5 minutes before transferring to a wire rack to finish cooling for at least 10 minutes before serving.

This dough will be slightly crumbly. Using wet hands helps keep it from sticking as you roll it into balls.

SERVING SIZE: 1 cookie

NUTRITION INFORMATION (PER SERVING): Calories: 113; Total Fat: 5 grams; Saturated Fat: 4 grams; Protein: 2 grams; Total Carbohydrates: 14 grams; Sugars: 7 grams; Fiber: 4 grams; Cholesterol: 27 milligrams; Sodium: 49 milligrams

Dulce de Leche Bowl

It drives me insane when my friends "ban" foods they love from their diet. There are so many tricks to lighten up favorites, especially sweets. You absolutely *can* enjoy ooey-gooey caramel. Swirl a small amount of the flavorful ingredient into Greek yogurt and sprinkle with chocolate chips—and enjoy!

Prep time: 10 minutes *Cook time:* 8 minutes SERVES 6

- 5 tablespoons granulated sugar
- 2 tablespoons unsalted butter
- 3 tablespoons heavy cream
- ½ teaspoon vanilla extract
- ⅛ teaspoon salt
- 2 cups nonfat vanilla Greek yogurt
- 6 tablespoons mini semisweet chocolate chips

Combine the sugar and butter in a small saucepan and cook over low heat, stirring continuously, until the mixture turns a light brown color, about 4 minutes. Add the heavy cream and stir. When the steam has dissipated, stir rapidly for about 1 full minute to combine the mixture. Then remove the pan from the heat, and stir in the vanilla extract and salt.

To assemble, place ⅓ cup of the yogurt in each of six bowls. Stir 4 teaspoons of the caramel sauce into each, and top with 1 tablespoon of the chocolate chips. Serve immediately.

SERVING SIZE: 1 bowl

NUTRITION INFORMATION (PER SERVING): Calories: 236; Total Fat: 11 grams; Saturated Fat: 7 grams; Protein: 9 grams; Total Carbohydrates: 26 grams; Sugars: 24 grams; Fiber: 0 grams; Cholesterol: 24 milligrams; Sodium: 97 milligrams

When making caramel, adding the cold heavy cream to the hot sugar and butter mixture will release steam. This is normal—don't panic!

Chocolate-Hazelnut Pudding Shooters

When I'm at a restaurant, the excessively large dessert portions are a pet peeve of mine. I always ask myself, why can't they make Toby-portioned treats? I took matters into my own hands and created these.

Prep time: 20 minutes *Cook time:* 12 minutes

SERVES 8

- ½ cup whole hazelnuts
- 1 cup nonfat vanilla Greek yogurt
- 2 ounces dark chocolate (60% to 70% cocoa)
- 2 tablespoons unsweetened cocoa powder
- 2 tablespoons confectioners' sugar

Preheat the oven to 350°F.

Place the hazelnuts on a baking sheet and toast in the oven for 10 minutes. Remove the baking sheet from the oven and set aside to cool slightly, about 10 minutes. Then wrap the toasted hazelnuts in a clean damp towel and rub them to remove their skins. Discard the skins. Chop the hazelnuts and set aside.

Place the yogurt in a medium bowl. Melt the chocolate in the microwave, about 90 seconds, stirring halfway through. Then stir the melted chocolate into the yogurt. Add the cocoa powder and confectioners' sugar, stirring until completely combined.

To assemble, place 1 tablespoon of the pudding into each of eight shot glasses, top it with ½ tablespoon of the chopped hazelnuts, and repeat the layers. Serve immediately or store in the refrigerator for up to 3 days.

SERVING SIZE: 1 shooter

NUTRITION INFORMATION (PER SERVING): Calories: 124; Total Fat: 8 grams; Saturated Fat: 2 grams; Protein: 5 grams; Total Carbohydrates: 10 grams; Sugars: 7 grams; Fiber: 2 grams; Cholesterol: 0 milligrams; Sodium: 12 milligrams

Hazelnuts contain high-quality protein and fiber, helping to keep you satisfied. They also provide a good dose of the antioxidant vitamin E and have a variety of plant chemicals shown to benefit the immune system.

Mojito Popsicles

The combination of chilled lemon, lime, and mint hits the spot on a blistering summer day. These citrus-flavored pops were a big hit with all ages, from my six-year-old critic to my toughest critic—my mom!

Prep time: 10 minutes, plus 4 hours in the freezer *Cook time:* 0 minutes MAKES 8 POPSICLES

- 1 cup plain almond milk
- ¾ cup nonfat lemon Greek yogurt
- 2 tablespoons grated lime zest
- ¼ cup fresh lime juice
- 1 tablespoon chopped fresh mint leaves

In a large bowl, whisk together the almond milk, yogurt, lime zest, lime juice, and mint. Pour into 12 standard-size ice pop molds, using a ¼-cup scoop, and insert a popsicle stick into each one. Freeze until set, at least 4 hours.

SERVING SIZE: 1 popsicle

NUTRITION INFORMATION (PER SERVING): Calories: 37; Total Fat: 1 gram; Saturated Fat: 0 grams; Protein: 3 grams; Total Carbohydrates: 5 grams; Sugars: 4 grams; Fiber: 0 grams; Cholesterol: 0 milligrams; Sodium: 23 milligrams

Panna Cotta Brûlée

Fire up your kitchen torch and put on protective eye gear! There's nothing more fun than caramelizing sugar to achieve that burnt, sweet flavor. You don't even need tons of sugar to do it—just a teaspoon or two will do the trick.

Prep time: 20 minutes, plus 4 hours refrigeration *Cook time:* 10 minutes SERVES 4

- 2 cups nonfat plain Greek yogurt
- ¼ cup plus 8 teaspoons superfine or regular granulated sugar
- 1 teaspoon vanilla extract
- ¾ cup low-fat milk
- 2 teaspoons unflavored gelatin powder

In a medium bowl, combine the yogurt, ¼ cup sugar, and vanilla extract. Set aside and allow the mixture to come to room temperature, about 15 minutes.

Meanwhile, pour the milk into a small saucepan off the stove, and sprinkle the gelatin over it. Set aside to allow the gelatin to soften, 5 minutes. Then place the pan over low heat to warm the milk and melt the gelatin, being sure not to let it boil. Stir until the gelatin has melted, 1 to 2 minutes.

Stir the warm milk mixture into the yogurt mixture and combine thoroughly. Pour about ½ cup of the mixture into each of four crème brûlée dishes or small bowls. Cover with plastic wrap and chill in the refrigerator until set, at least 4 hours or up to 12 hours.

Just before serving, sprinkle 2 teaspoons of the remaining sugar over each panna cotta. Then immediately use a kitchen torch to carefully caramelize the sugar. Serve.

SERVING SIZE: 1 panna cotta

NUTRITION INFORMATION (PER SERVING): Calories: 172; Total Fat: 0 grams; Saturated Fat: 0 grams; Protein: 15 grams; Total Carbohydrates: 28 grams; Sugars: 28 grams; Fiber: 0 grams; Cholesterol: 2 milligrams; Sodium: 79 milligrams

Notes

1. *Wall Street Journal.* "Old Factory, Snap Decision Spawn Greek-Yogurt Craze." Available at http://online.wsj.com/article/SB10001424052702303379204577476974123310582.html. Accessed July 31, 2013.
2. Packaged Facts. "The Yogurt Market and Yogurt Innovation: Greek Yogurt and Beyond." Available at http://www.slideshare.net/MarketResearchcom/the-yogurt-market-and-yogurt-innovation-sample. Accessed October 25, 2013.
3. U.S. Department of Agriculture National Nutrient Database for Standard Reference Release 26. Available at http://ndb.nal.usda.gov/. Accessed October 26, 2013.
4. U.S. Department of Health and Human Services and U.S. Department of Agriculture. "Dietary Guidelines for Americans, 2010." Available at http://www.health.gov/dietaryguidelines/dga2010/DietaryGuidelines2010.pdf. Accessed October 26, 2013.
5. J. Saikali, C. Picard, M. Freitas, and P. Holt. "Fermented Milks, Probiotic Cultures, and Colon Cancer," *Nutrition and Cancer* 49, no. 1 (2004): 14–24.
6. National Heart, Lung and Blood Institute. Available at http://www.nhlbi.nih.gov. Accessed August 7, 2013.
7. M. C. Houston and K. J. Harper. "Potassium, magnesium, and calcium: their role in both the cause and treatment of hypertension." *Journal of Clinical Hypertension* (Greenwich) 10, no. 7 Suppl. (July 2008): 3–11.
8. K L. Ivey, J. R. Lewis, J. M. Hodgson, K. Zhu, S. S. Dhaliwal, P. L. Thompson, and R. L. Prince. "Association between yogurt, milk, and cheese consumption and common carotid artery intima-media thickness and cardiovascular disease risk factors in elderly women." *American Journal of Clinical Nutrition* 94, no. 1 (July 2011): 234–239.
9. L. Djousse, J. S. Panko, S. C. Hunt, et al. "Influence of saturated fat and linoleic acid on the association between intake of dairy products and blood pressure." *Hypertension* 48 (2006):335–341.
10. A. Alonso, J. J. Beunza, M. Delgado-Rodriguez, J. A. Martinez, and M. A. Martinez-Gonzalez. "Low-fat dairy consumption and reduced risk of hypertension: the Seguimiento Universidad de Navarra (SUN) cohort." *American Journal of Clinical Nutrition* 82, no. 5 (Nov. 2005): 972–978.
11. D. R. Shahar, D. Schwarzfuchs, D. Fraser, et al. "Dairy calcium intake, serum vitamin D, and successful weight loss." *American Journal of Clinical Nutrition* 92, no. 5 (Nov. 2010): 1017–1022.
12. M. B. Zemel, J. Richards, S. Mathis, A. Milstead, L. Gebhardt, and E. Silva. "Dairy augmentation of total and central fat

loss in obese subjects." *International Journal of Obesity* (London) 29, no. 4 (April 2006): 391–397.

13. M. S. Eagan, M. N. Lyle, C. W. Gunther, et al. "Effect of a 1-year dairy product intervention on fat mass in young women: 6-month follow-up." *Obesity* 14 (2006): 2242–2248.
14. T. J. Key, P. N. Appleby, E. A. Spencer, A. W. Roddam, R. E. Neale, and N. E. Allen. "Calcium, diet and fracture risk: a prospective study of 1898 incident fractures among 34,696 British women and men." *Public Health Nutrition* 10 (2007): 1314–1320.
15. National Institute of Child Health and Human Development. "How Much Calcium Do Kids Need?" Available at http://www.nichd.nih.gov/milk/prob/Pages/calcium_need.aspx. Accessed October 26, 2013.
16. S. Liu, A. Klevak, H. K. Choi, et al. "A prospective study of dairy intake and the risk of type 2 diabetes in women." *Diabetes Care* 29 (2006): 1579
17. H. K. Choi, W. C. Willett, M. J. Stampfer, et al. "Dairy consumption and risk of type 2 diabetes mellitus in men: a prospective study." *Archives of Internal Medicine* 165 (2005): 997.
18. L. Getz. "On track with a snack." *Today's Dietitian* 12, no. 9 (Sept. 2010): 32.

Metric Conversion Chart

Use these charts as a guideline. In the United States, recipe ingredient lists are usually based on volume, rather than weight. Baking recipes (breads, muffins, cakes) do require precision, so exact conversions are necessary.

U.S. TO METRIC CONVERSION, VOLUME (DRY AND LIQUID)	
U.S.	*Metric*
¼ teaspoon	1 milliliters
½ teaspoon	2 milliliters
1 teaspoon	5 milliliters
1 fluid ounce (2 tablespoons)	30 milliliters
2 fluid ounces (¼ cup)	60 milliliters
8 fluid ounces (1 cup)	240 milliliters
16 fluid ounces (1 pint)	480 milliliters
32 fluid ounces (1 quart)	950 milliliters (0.95 liter)
128 fluid ounces (1 gallon)	3.75 liters

U.S. TO METRIC CONVERSION, VOLUME (LIQUID)	
Fluid Ounces	*Milliliters*
1	30
2	60
3	90
4	120
5	150
6	180
7	210
8	240

U.S. TO METRIC CONVERSION, WEIGHT	
U.S.	*Metric (rounded)*
½ ounce	15 grams
1 ounce	30 grams
4 ounces	115 grams
8 ounces (½ pound)	225 grams
16 ounces (1 pound)	450 grams
32 ounces (2 pounds)	900 grams

U.S. TO METRIC CONVERSION CHART, TEMPERATURE	
Degrees Fahrenheit	*Degrees Celsius*
325	163
350	177
375	191
400	204
425	218
450	232
475	246

U.S. CONVERSIONS, VOLUME
3 teaspoons = 1 tablespoon
2 tablespoons = 1 fluid ounce
8 fluid ounces = 1 cup
2 cups = 1 pint
2 pints = 1 quart
4 quarts = 1 gallon

IMPERIAL CONVERSIONS, VOLUME
10 fluid ounces Imperial = 1 cup
20 fluid ounces Imperial = 1 pint
40 fluid ounces Imperial = 1 quart

Index

About the Author

Toby Amidor, MS, RD, CDN, is the founder of Toby Amidor Nutrition, through which she provides nutrition and food safety consulting services. She serves as the nutrition expert for FoodNetwork.com and writes for its Healthy Eats blog; serves as a nutrition advisor for Sears' FitStudio.com, an online fitness community; and serves as an adjunct professor at Teachers College, Columbia University in New York City. Toby is also a contributor to the *U.S. News & World Report* Eat + Run blog and has a monthly column in *Today's Dietitian* magazine. She is a nutrition consultant for seasons two, three, and four of Bobby Deen's *Not My Mama's Meals,* airing on the Cooking Channel.

In 2012 Toby became a member of the National Dairy Council's Lactose Intolerance Speakers Bureau. In 2013 she authored a chapter in a college textbook, *Food Science, An Ecological Approach*, titled "Milk, Cheese and Dairy Replacements." Toby also contributed to the chapter entitled "Know Your Ingredients" in the 1997 edition of *The All New Joy of Cooking.* She has appeared in media outlets including *Woman's World* magazine, Parents.com, Fitbie.com, CNN .com, Yahoo! Shine, *Good Morning America Health, Good Day New York, Self* magazine, *U.S. Weekly* magazine, WebMD.com, *Pregnancy & Newborn* magazine, *Working Mother* magazine, the *New York Daily News, Fitness* magazine, and the *Journal of the Academy of Nutrition and Dietetics.*

For thirteen years, Toby taught aspiring chefs about nutrition, food safety, and restaurant management at the Art Institute of New York City. Toby has done private nutrition counseling in Bronx, New York, focusing on childhood obesity, and was a dietitian at New York Methodist Hospital in Brooklyn, New York.

Toby trained as a clinical dietitian at New York University and has more than fourteen years of experience in various areas of food and nutrition. Through her ongoing consulting and faculty positions, she has established herself as one of the top experts in culinary nutrition and food safety.